Knightsbridge
Woman

By the same author

The Word of a Prince

Knightsbridge Woman

Maria Perry

illustrations by
Bernard Cookson

ANDRE DEUTSCH

First published in Great Britain in 1995 by
André Deutsch Limited
106 Great Russell Street
London WC1B 3LJ

CIP data for this title is available from the British Library.

ISBN 0 233 98940 4

Phototypeset by Intype, London
Printed in Great Britain by WBC Bridgend

For Julian

Contents

ACKNOWLEDGEMENTS

Ms Carrie Starren of the Royal Borough of Kensington & Chelsea's Local History Library; Lieutenant Colonel Hamon Massey, formerly Commanding Officer of the Household Cavalry Mounted Regiment; Mr Neil Mitchell of the Royal Parks Equitation Trust; Miss Sophie Laybourne of *The Daily Telegraph* Fashion Page; Mrs Carole Seymour-Newton of the Knightsbridge Association and Mr Michael Cole and the staff of Harrods' Press Office, and Archives Department.

1

The Grocer's

FOUR ROYAL APPOINTMENTS emblazoned against the rose brick façade of Harrods proclaim the virtues of the mighty London store. They reveal to an enthralled public the shopping habits of the House of Windsor. Beneath the lion and the unicorn supporting the arms of Her Majesty the Queen is the simple legend 'Suppliers of Provisions and Households Goods'. This cuts Harrods down to size. To Her Majesty, as to the thousands of discerning spenders to whom this book is dedicated, the most famous shop in the world is still the local grocer's.

'Outfitters' in gold letters under the 'D' in Duke and the 'd' in Edinburgh affirms Prince Philip's interest. A royal equerry might drop in for a handy pair of socks.

Our beloved Queen Mother's warrant confesses her passion for 'China, Glass and Fancy Goods' while, to the Prince of Wales, Harrods offers a dual service as 'Outfitters and Saddlers'. It is puzzling to think that a man who lives in rural Gloucestershire might send all the way to sw1 for a spare girth, but reassuring that HRH, a former pupil of Hill House in Hans Place, should still buy clothes from the shop which supplied his first school uniform. Some people worry dreadfully about a future King of England shopping in a men's wear department crammed with Armani suits, French underpants and drip-dry shirts labelled 'Eton – Made in Sweden', but the Prince has not been sighted in such gear. His own shirtmakers, Turnbull & Asser of Jermyn Street, have even opened a shop within a shop on Harrods' ground floor.

German tourists are often baffled to see Prince Charles's motto, *Ich dien* – I serve – displayed prominently above Harrods' side door. It has led a few to suppose that now we have gone helter-skelter into Europe, they might find the Heir Apparent behind the bacon counter, working to pay his mother's Income Tax.

Amidst the mottoes on the royal appointments, however, Prince Philip's stands out most clearly. It is in plain English and voices the feelings of every man in the land whose mother, daughter, wife or mistress ever held a green and gold Harrods account card. It says quite simply, 'God is my help'.

2

Shopping

SHOPPING IS THE universal pursuit of the Knights-bridge classes. One of the chief charms of the place is that you can shop there with money or without it.

I first discovered this on a chilly September morning in the seventies, when I arrived in London from Djakarta, shivering in tropical clothing and clutching a purse of Indonesian rupiahs. My only other currency was a cheque-book drawable on the Svenska Handelsbanken. Early Eurocrats, we lived in Stockholm, retaining a Kensington *pied-à-terre* for sentimental reasons. While we were abroad it had been illegally sublet to a Norwegian weaver, who taught at the Royal College of Art. Her students reckoned she was clairvoyant.

On this occasion she appeared at Heathrow, waving the keys to our flat, just as I, nostalgic for the green fields of England, decided to get off a plane bound for Scandinavia. My luggage, labelled in perfect Swedish, was whisked efficiently through Customs and not seen again for two months, after which it turned up intact at Victoria Station. With a mystic gleam in her eye the Norwegian lady swept me into a waiting car and dumped me at my own front door. She then disappeared to Tunbridge Wells for the weekend, taking all her spare cardigans with her.

I had been away from London for four years. When I searched my cupboards I found only a selection of looms and some tall spools of coloured wool. Eventually a hat-box disgorged a bikini, some kid gloves and a long-forgotten Harrods account card. Whooping like some victorious member of the Sioux tribe, I set off through Hyde Park to walk to Knightsbridge. Hours later I returned, swaddled in seasonal cashmere.

3

Where is Knightsbridge?

THIS SIMPLE QUESTION has baffled many cartographers. For the convenience of visitors to London, we feel we should dwell on a few of the eccentricities which make English place names unique.

On a modern map Knightsbridge is a brief stretch of road south of Hyde Park, running approximately from Hyde Park Corner to Rutland Gate. It boasts three five-star hotels (*four* if you count the Berkeley, which is more a way of life), five ladies' hairdressers, its own underpass, its own cinema and a minimum of residential property. Its assets include the French and Kuwaiti Embassies, the Royal Thames Yacht Club, the Pizza on the Park, an accredited gambling casino and a complete unit of the Household Cavalry.

Apart from the bit where daffodils bloom each spring behind the No. 9 bus stop it is a concrete jungle, but a jungle famed internationally for its affluence and chic. Some of the best-dressed women in the world come to buy clothes in this golden half-mile. It is no place for shrinking violets. Competition is fierce and Knightsbridge Woman after a sale bargain is inclined to be red in tooth and claw. Irrespective of age or nationality, what she wants she usually gets, and Knightsbridge Woman after a parking place on Saturday morning is the most fearsome adversary known to mankind. Tall or short, plump or slim, blonde or brunette, determination is the hallmark of the breed.

Knightsbridge proper sells coats and suits, frocks and shoes. It is deeply concerned with *lifestyles*. To prove the point, when Harvey Nichols opened their new food department they gave away a brochure featuring a nude model, entirely wrapped in *al dente* spaghetti. At Knightsbridge Green, however, Burberrys and The Scotch House still comfortingly purvey raincoats and cardigans, tartans and tweed, while *haute couture* in gem-like colours prevails from the Sloane Street traffic lights to the tip of Wilton Crescent. In Knightsbridge all tastes are catered for; it even boasts two lingerie shops – Bradleys, long-established and frothing with cream lace for the trousseaux of Easter brides, and Rose Lewis, where the international set are said to drop in when they want to buy 'something different'. At Bradleys ladies of majestic proportions can still order made-to-measure housecoats, and a stately clientèle of discerning duchesses send for silk camisoles and thermal vests at the start of the autumn to offset the draughts in Border Castles.

Rose specialises more. Her window displays are lush with black satin and spangled G-strings. Occasionally they take the whole district by surprise. There are sporadic little outbursts of high camp that cause passengers on the normally staid No. 9 bus to crane their necks for a surreptitious thrill. Arab ladies wafting by on a demure errand to the Al-Kashkool Bookshop have been known to stop in their tracks and giggle behind their veils, while high-minded mothers, shopping for debutantes at the start of the Season, hurry their daughters past in a sort of conspiratorial silence. 'I think', said a titled matron from the Shires, dubiously eyeing two New York cross-dressers coveting the same purple thong, 'that these undies can't be meant for *English* people.'

So much for Knightsbridge itself. As a general area it spreads far beyond the dusty stretch of road, though it is a good deal harder to pinpoint. 'Difficult of definition' grumbles the *Companion Guide to London*, but with two main focuses: one at the junction with Sloane Street, where Harvey Nichols faces the exuberant splendours of the Hyde Park Hotel, and a second, '*the deep heart-beat of the region*' some hundred yards south-west where Harrods occupies a whole block of the Brompton Road. This off-centre location has never troubled Harrods. In 1921, by special arrangement with the Post Office, they changed their address to 'Knightsbridge' and in Knightsbridge they have continued to stand for the past seventy-four years with flamboyant disregard for the 'Brompton Road' street sign, which the Royal Borough of Kensington and Chelsea has painstakingly fixed above the tube exit.

In the London A-Z 'Knightsbridge' is marked three times, creating instant confusion for the map reader. Let us imagine that, late for a dinner party, she is trying to dry her nail varnish in the fan heater of a motor car, while simultaneously directing her mate to an address in Ennismore Mews. Bobbing before her on the page, as the car takes the S-bend in Kensington Church Street, the word 'Knightsbridge' marks the road, the tube station and, in heavy type, an imposing wedge of territory stretching from Kensington Gore to Belgravia. This includes the Albert Hall, but cuts out Sloane Street altogether. The A-Z also severely distinguishes Knightsbridge from Brompton, which baffles casual shoppers who thought they were one and the same. Cognoscenti and natives of course know that Brompton has only recently 'come up', having managed to shed that aura of shabbiness which clung to it from Victorian times, deeply upsetting Cardinal Newman when the London Oratory was being planned. 'That suburb,' he called it witheringly, 'that neighbourhood of second-rate gentry and second-rate shops.'

Time was to prove him terribly wrong. Postally Knightsbridge spans two very chic districts, sw1 and sw7 – *three*, if you count the hinterland of Beauchamp Place which, though technically Brompton, is spiritually Knightsbridge, despite being postcoded sw3. (This, as any Londoner will tell you, makes it irrefutably Chelsea.)

Beauchamp Place is the Mecca of shoppers who are *real* Ladies. In the sacred pursuit of Thrift, they sweep up from the country in chauffeur-driven Bentleys at the start of the Season, vowing their sole intention is to replenish the Spode at the Reject China Shop. Should they get sidetracked into Bruce Oldfield, Sarah Spencer, Janet Reger, Caroline Charles, Paddy Campbell or Annabel Jones, that is just 'savoir faire'. 'Temptation', if a killjoy husband chances to find the bill.

Real ladies own some of the shops, too. Lady Tryon sells frocks at No. 3 Beauchamp Place, under the sign of 'Kanga', a nickname given her by the Prince of Wales.

'That suburb,' he called it witheringly, 'that neighbourhood of second-rate gentry and second-rate shops.'

On the other side of the street 'Annabel Jones' is really the maiden name of Lady Astor, who started her jewellery business in a corner of the Brompton Arcade, until overnight fame caused her to take smarter premises. Caroline Charles and Janet Reger are not *real* Ladies, but they are real people. So much grandeur has rubbed off on the shopkeepers, accustomed as they are to high-class patronage and exposure on the front cover of *Vogue*, that when Sarah Spencer opened up to sell evening wear at No. 26 (a stone's throw from the Princess of Wales's favourite restaurant, San Lorenzo) everyone assumed she must be a royal relation. The narrow stairs were immediately jammed with ardent shoppers. Most were too discreet or too well-bred to enquire. The dresses are lovely, but Sarah herself does not exist; the trade name was a happy invention.

If you now feel you are beginning to get to grips with the *ethos* of Knightsbridge, you may well be right. But if you think this means you know where it is, dear reader, we must warn you that you are probably wide of the mark. Politically Knightsbridge is not at all where you have been led to believe. Half of it lies in the Royal Borough of Kensington and Chelsea, the rest is in the City of Westminster. Study the ward maps which both Councils pin up in their public libraries and you will find the triangle so confidently labelled KNIGHTSBRIDGE in the A-Z is no such place. Officially it is HANS TOWN. This is in pious memory of Sir Hans Sloane, who acquired the Manor of Chelsea in 1712. Harrods and the tube station lie in Hans Town, while the ward of Knightsbridge itself skims the top of Belgrave Square, veers crazily up

West Halkin Street and leaps northwards into Hyde Park. This irritates many Belgravians who, deeming themselves superior, hate to see anything as downmarket as 'Knightsbridge' on the polling forms.

4

Great Developers

Q UITE A FEW QUEENS of England have been shopa-
holics, but the original Knightsbridge Woman was
surely Mary II, whose husband bought her Kensington Palace and built her Rotten Row. Styled 'Route
du Roi', it joined William III's new house at Kensington
with the Palace of Whitehall. Historians say the King
built it to speed up state business, but trained royal watch-
ers know he had a deeper motive. Leaf through Queen
Mary's shopping lists and it becomes quite obvious that
Rotten Row was built *wide* to carry all the packages.

Mary had that really vicious shopper's habit of buying
things in quantity and thinking up a use for them after
the event. She ordered satin slippers by the dozen and
had a standing order with her glovemaker for twenty-four
pairs a month. She bought hundreds of yards of ribbon at
a time, and her taste in lingerie was avant-garde to say
the least. For the Queen of England wore black embroidered stays and red and white striped negligées. She was
constantly buying little presents for William in the bazaar.
On one occasion she visited a bawdyhouse (an easy mistake in her day, as the Curiosity Shop was often a front
for quite another sort of business). When the story got

about that Mary and all her ladies had been taking tea in a brothel, William said, 'Next time you go to such a place, it is only proper that I should be of the party.'

William and Mary were Great Developers. From the moment the English invited the Dutch Prince to be their King instead of the unsatisfactory James II, William was determined to change things. Rotten Row was the first road in London to have street lighting. William hung three hundred lamps along it since the notorious village of Knightsbridge lay nearby and it was full of highwaymen and footpads. The lighting had absolutely no effect on the crime rate, for the highwaymen, attracted by the rich pickings from courtiers travelling from Westminster to Kensington, redoubled their efforts. Right up to the nineteenth century persons walking from Westminster to Kensington travelled in bands for protection.

William bought his new house from the Earl of Nottingham in 1689 for £28,000. The King suffered dreadfully from asthma and Kensington, a village only two miles from the capital, was noted for its healthy air. When they first arrived from Holland, Mary felt neurotically confined at Whitehall, where she complained she could see only 'water and wall'. Superstitious maids of honour were also prone to sighting Charles I's headless ghost. Everyone grew fearfully nervous. River mists from the Thames made William's condition worse and finally constant smog, from the sea-coal fires with which the Londoners heated their houses, drove the couple to modernise Hampton Court.

Like all Great Developers William and Mary were fussy. Sir Christopher Wren was chosen for the job. William told him to knock down the old Tudor palace and create a mini-Versailles, but parliament mumbled about finance. Wren modified his plans. William, who was no conservationist, thought he had done a botch job. The King also found Hampton Court too far out of Town. Critics reckoned he should have left it alone and refurbished St James's Palace. It had been good enough for five generations of British monarchs, they argued, so it should have suited a *Dutchman*. Alas, it must have reminded poor William uncomfortably of his wedding night, when his merry uncle, Charles II, had drawn back the bed curtains on the newly-married couple, crying, 'Now, nephew, to your work! Hey! St George for England!'

Kensington was soon chosen as the main royal home with its healthy air and lack of embarrassing associations.

Queen Mary was a homebody. The daughter of a more than usually scandalous Duchess of York, Anne Hyde, she had been brought up very carefully at the Court of her Uncle Charles, who died woefully short of legitimate issue. Mary inherited a streak of almost bourgeois simplicity from her grandfather, Sir Edward Hyde, the Lord Chancellor of England. When he discovered his daughter was pregnant by the King's amorous brother, the Duke of York, Sir Edward called for an Act of Parliament to have her executed. 'I am not obliged', he said, bursting into tears, 'to keep a whore for the greatest Prince alive.'

Charles II told him not to be silly. All passion should be set aside and the pair must be married at once. Visualising the scandal that would arise and that he, a member of the Middle Classes, would be accused of *networking* to get his own issue on the throne, the Chancellor wept afresh and begged the King to send his daughter to the

'Now, nephew, to your work! Hey! St George for England!'

Tower. It then emerged that the couple had already married in secret, so the baby, a boy, was born in wedlock after all. There followed Mary and her sister Anne. The boy child died, but Uncle Charles saw to it that as legitimate royal issue the girls were brought up as God-fearing members of the Church of England. Indeed Mary was so pious that at her own coronation she thought the pomp and ceremony detracted from the importance of Holy Communion, which she and the King were about to take in Westminster Abbey. This did not deter her from ordering a new crown, and having it set with the largest diamond in Europe.

Maybe it was because her mother had such a bad time in pregnancy, or maybe it was the suspicion that William had a mistress that drove Queen Mary to shopping. One of the small nagging worries of her life was that she could never quite manage her pin money.

'I can't tell how it has been laid out,' she would write across her accounts, 'but I know 'tis all gone.'

She alternated fits of economy, like having a cloak re-lined, with bouts of extravagance, such as rebuilding Hampton Court and deciding not to live there.

Kensington gave her great scope. With Wren and Hawksmoor as builders she set out to create a homely atmosphere, where she and William could take tea. She was so keen to leave Whitehall that in 1690 she went almost daily to Kensington to 'hasten the workmen'. In the end the Royal Family moved in before the builders moved out. Wren had to put up pavilions to accommodate all the staff. As soon as the palace was finished Queen Mary indulged her twin passions for gardening and

[16]

collecting curios. She furnished Kensington Palace with East India calicoes and chintzes. She also collected blue and white delft, and porcelain from China.

Soon the palace was full to overflowing, causing the Queen to have cupboards and shelves designed to display her trophies. Chinaware was piled upon cabinets and escritoires and every chimney-piece to the ceilings. The Queen had set a new fashion and the nobility and gentry were quick to take it up. All over England people started collecting blue and white china, piling it upon mantel-pieces until it became a grievance.

'The expence of it', wrote Defoe, was 'even injurious to families and estates', although he was quick to add that it was not Mary's *fault*, since she had no idea that she was 'laying the foundation for such fatal excesses' and would no doubt have been the first to have reformed them had she lived to see it. Defoe, and others, thought the passion for lolling about in rooms cluttered with blue and white jugs would end in the downfall of a great nation. An Act of Parliament was passed to limit the import of chintzes and the country went back to healthy English ways of squandering money – at the card tables and the racecourse.

5

Parking

OBLIVIOUS TO THE NEEDS of daytime shoppers, the boundary line between Kensington and Westminster slices through Knightsbridge creating mayhem for the owner driver. Take for example Montpelier Street, where the elegant navy blue meters beside Bonhams, the auctioneers, belong to the Royal Borough, while the functional black ones opposite are the property of the City of Westminster. On dull days the colours are indistinguishable, but to park on the Kensington side costs £1.60 an hour, while across the street the fee is £2.

There is no regional variation in the excess fines. Both authorities charge £60 for the sin of idling five minutes too long in, let us say, the Patisserie Gloriette, or for dallying over the cut of a blazer in Emporio Armani, but to encourage prompt payment there is a 50 per cent discount available to those settling their accounts within fourteen days. It is still marginally cheaper to park in Kensington, and the morning scramble for the navy blue meters resembles the last lap at Le Mans. Losers park on the black side, where the air is rent with horrible expletives.

Now that the job has been let out to private tender,

two different companies, Sureway and Parktel, manage the meters. On the Bonhams side the Royal Borough clothes its wardens in smart khaki uniforms with forest green ties and forage caps, which give them the air of belonging to an elite guerilla corps. The Westminster mob are rigged less threateningly in familiar navy blue, but they have recently perfected a new technique of gazing nonchalantly into shop windows as though they were ordinary pedestrians, then slyly leaping out to time a meter from the instant an unsuspecting driver walks away.

It is a well-known fact that the Westminster wardens are a ruthless breed, so for the protection of its own residents renewing parking permits, the Royal Borough has taken to sending out little maps showing the boundary line in all its wild eccentricity. First it divides Queen's Gate down the middle, granting a strange dual residency to the equestrian statue of Lord Napier. Then it sidles along the backside of the Imperial College of Science and Technology, runs amok near Ennismore Mews, and meanders off towards the French Embassy. Woe betide the K & C permit holder who parks in Kensington Gore, carelessly fooled by the name into believing she is on home ground. The mistake is common. It accounts for a large part of the earned income paid out by the Home Office and the two local authorities to the TRACE clamping units.

Lowndes Square is another high risk area. At Albert Gate the boundary line erratically makes a right angle turn and drops due south. This leaves the west, or Harvey Nicks' side of the square for cars bearing K & C permits, while residents of the eastern block may only park in spaces labelled with the City of Westminster's imposing capital 'A'. Spaces for diplomats' cars are reserved at diagonally opposite ends of the square, beside the Pakistani Embassy and by Caroline Dickenson's flower shop. These present additional hazards to the casual motorist cruising the square in search of neutral territory in which to 'Pay and Display'.

Foreign visitors or country shoppers, who cause obstruction by putting cars in the south-west corner of the square, may be clamped or towed way by officers from the Chelsea Police Station.* Offenders in the north-east corner are more likely to be answerable to the Belgravia Division in their smart, new headquarters in Buckingham Palace Road. Vigilantes from both stations patrol the square in identical vans, decorated with the Met's distinctive black and white chequerboard pattern. As a one-way system operates in Lowndes Square, they frequently overlap, putting the hapless motorist in double jeopardy. Even the natives cannot cope, and punters at the Park Tower Casino should budget an extra £105 on top of their gambling losses for clamping and tow away fees.

As the square is a handy parking spot for Harvey Nichols account customers, for patrons of Valentino, and Gucci Sloane Street, it has become a popular local spectator sport to count the confiscated Rolls-Royces being towed away on Saturday mornings. When Harvey Nicks or Gucci Sloane Street announce a sale, the Kent and

---

*Recently re-named the 'Brompton Division', a piece of wilful bureaucracy which native Londoners rightly ignore.

[20]

Sussex Brigade rush up to nab a bargain and lunch in Basil Street at the Parrot Club. A few rash souls always attempt double parking. This brings out officers from the new Belgravia Division in droves, panting to use the millions of pounds' worth of computerised equipment with which they have been issued to monitor traffic flow.

The creation of the Belgravia Division caused instant uproar. It brought about the closure of the élite Gerald Road Police Station, which was just beside the home of the late Sir Noël Coward. Such passionate nostalgia was aroused in the breasts of local residents that *The Times* ran a special column on the Letters Page, and the Home Office was deluged with protests from Peers of the Realm and High Court Judges. Gerald Road was famed for the tact of its officers and the beauty of its window boxes. At the opening of the shiny new HQ, so expensively updated to beat the Crime Wave, the Home Office was obliged to pledge that there would be *no* decline in *the standards of Police horticulture*.

6

Her One Extravagance

ACCORDING TO LEGEND Knightsbridge took its name from a stone bridge where two knights fought to the death. It would be marvellous to relate that they quarrelled over a Woman, but the cause of their unholy row is lost in the mists of time. We know only that it broke out when they were on their way to seek a blessing from the Bishop of London before setting off on that most bloody of Christian adventures – a Crusade.

The bridge belonged to the Abbot of Westminster, who leased a bit of Hyde Park from the Crown. It crossed the River Westbourne, which seeped out of the Park where Albert Gate now stands. Today it runs underground, roughly one hundred yards west of Harvey Nichols' cosmetics department. The river was diverted through a pipe by a celebrated feat of eighteenth-century engineering. Such a pity. If it had stayed where it was, separating the parish of St Margaret's Westminster from that of St George's Hanover Square, it would have made the parking arrangements so much clearer, and put an end to the dreadful muddle outside Harvey Nicks on Saturday morning.

The culprit in all this was one of England's most

amiable Queens, Caroline of Ansbach, who moved the Westbourne to make room for the Serpentine, and built the Round Pond to improve the view. Wife to the irascible George II, she was known as 'Caroline the Good'. She had a trying time amid the general turbulence of Hanoverian family life, but she was the type who loyally stuck by her husband through thick and thin. As Princess of Wales, she took his side in a sordid squabble with her father-in-law, George I, who called her a 'she-devil', and, as Queen of England, she generously made her husband's mistress, Lady Suffolk, her Mistress of the Robes. Indeed Caroline managed to stay on good terms with almost everyone, the exception being her eldest son, Frederick, Prince of Wales, who was universally detested and went down in English History as 'Poor Fred'.

Had she lived in our own time, Caroline would certainly have needed a therapist, for when he was really worked up George II indulged in fearful fits of wig-throwing, and the sight of her consort systematically demolishing the locks his valet had curled and powdered that very morning must have torn the poor woman's nerves to shreds. No wonder she took to landscape gardening.

The Queen had a passion for water. No city could contain enough of it for her. Nurtured at Herrenhausen, a German Schloss famous for its tinkling fountains, she set about improving Kensington Palace as soon as she moved in. Queen Anne in her forthright manner had ripped up her sister's Dutch Garden, because the smell of box hedges reminded her of cat's pee. She replaced it with a plantation which was just starting to grow when Caroline tore up the newly set saplings and sent in a squad of brawny

[23]

George II indulged in fearful fits of wig-throwing.

workmen to dig the Round Pond. In this she was shame-lessly encouraged by her husband's Prime Minister, Sir Robert Walpole, who shared her mania for gardening and got parliament to fix her up with a jointure of £100,000 – a bigger private income than had been enjoyed by any previous Queen of England. As Caroline's taste was for hard-wearing velvet and ermine, as she wore modest wigs and had a versatile way with her pearls, twisting them in her hair to save on tiaras, parliament reckoned she could be trusted not to go spending on frippery. They had overlooked the gardening.

Despite his dazzling career in public life, Sir Robert Walpole saw himself as a classicist manqué. He had been forced to cut short his studies at Cambridge owing to the untimely death of his older brother. Obliged to manage his father's estates at a time when he should have been translating Virgil's *Eclogues*, he developed a disconcerting habit in later life of reciting poetry to anyone who cared to listen. As the Queen was a bit of a blue-stocking too, the pair quickly hatched a contingency plan for dealing with the King's bad temper.

At the slightest sign that George was about to start wig-throwing Caroline would withdraw for a stroll round the Round Pond, swapping Latin odes with Sir Robert. Scandalmongers of the day spread spiteful stories that she dreamed up the Serpentine just so that she and the Prime Minister could dally longer over their hexameters.

The Queen bought up three hundred acres of Hyde Park as a handy site for her garden extension. Even Sir Robert thought this was going a bit far. He told Caroline that tampering with the landscape of Hyde Park might cost her the Crown. Accustomed as a child to hearing George II's imperious old grandmother, the Electress Sophia, dispute Problems of Time and Space with the philosopher Leibnitz, she was not, as Queen of England, going to have her style cramped by the prejudices of parliament and a Norfolk Squire. She scooped up the eleven little pools which made Hyde Park into a marshy wilderness, and promptly created London's largest artificial lake.

Being German, the Queen went into everything beforehand with great thoroughness. She *costed* the project with her gardener, Charles Bridgman, and roped in the Surveyor General of Woods and Forests, Charles Withers. They came up with a budget of £6,000. George II was delighted. The new lake would make such a pretty backdrop to the carriage road he was building, and as the Queen promised to pay for the work from her jointure it wasn't going to cost him a penny. United in their schemes for home improvement, husband and wife pooh-poohed Sir Robert's baleful warnings.

Unfortunately Caroline encountered one or two Problems of Time and Space. As the Westbourne formed part of London's main water supply, it had to be pumped by an atmospheric steam engine into a reservoir near Ranelagh Gardens. Stands were built so that an admiring populace could watch this remarkable public event. Before the Serpentine was completed, the Surveyor of Woods and Forests died. He had kept tight control of the purse strings, but had overlooked the fact that part of the Westbourne had been leased to the Chelsea Water Works Company at an annual rent of 6s 8d. They held a ninety-nine-year lease. The company demanded compensation, which swallowed half the royal budget.

When Caroline died she left George II desolate. She also left him to pick up a tab of £20,000 construction arrears for the Serpentine. This may have accounted for the King's strange behaviour at her death bed. As Caroline's last hour approached, she turned tenderly to her weeping spouse and told him that he must re-marry. 'Non,' sobbed the monarch hoarsely. 'J'aurai des maitresses.'

7

The Ladies of England

CAROLINE OF ANSBACH has a lot to answer for. She never stopped to consider what effect her passion for water might have upon future generations. For the convenience of the Royal Family two yachts were berthed in the Serpentine, while the Round Pond was soon to become a popular spot for small boys to sail their model boats. This led to a succession of Dukes of York being inspired to join the Navy, where several of them picked up coarse language and took to drinking rum. The rum was free before battle. Soon the whole nation was awash with sea-going ambition. George II, spotting the Duchess of Bedford dashing through Hyde Park in a dark blue riding habit, hit on the idea of dressing his sailors in Navy Blue to distinguish them from the army. The foundations of British sartorial taste were laid for centuries to come.

Previous sovereigns had hunted in Hyde Park. Henry VIII and Elizabeth I held military tattoos there. Charles I brought in flat racing, and Charles II paraded Nell Gwyn. She was followed by a dazzling selection of his other mistresses, and the Park quickly became a centre of fashion. Vying to outdress each other, decked in silks and satins, their hats billowing with unsuitable plumes, the ladies of England were driven about in chaises and curricles while their menfolk practised dangerous equestrian skills. Duels had always taken place with monotonous regularity, but there had never before been water. At any rate not in the quantities provided by Caroline. Its effect on the English sporting character was sensational. The Duke of Cumberland took to yachting so avidly that he raced a whole squadron up and down the Thames.

In severe winters the Serpentine froze over hard enough for skating, which brought about a flurry of new fashions in bonnets and pelisses, while in the hard winter of 1826 Mr Henry Hunt drove a coach and four across the ice for a stake of 100 guineas. In the nineteenth century impetuous skaters were always having to be rescued, through rushing onto the ice before it had frozen properly. The Serpentine also became a favourite haunt for prospective suicides. The most celebrated was Harriet Shelley, first wife of the poet, who drowned herself there in 1816. It was not really surprising: Shelley, an avant-garde Etonian who disapproved of Royalty, meat-eating and the Church of England, had just run off with the seventeen-year-old Mary Godwin (who later wrote *Frankenstein*).

Throughout the eighteenth century the Palace Gardens were open to the public on Saturdays, when the Court went to Kew. They were posh from the outset: visitors were required to put on full dress to walk there, carriages had to be left at the gate, and servants and dogs were banned. This explains the different vibes which sensitive New Age souls pick up when, after practising Yoga or T'ai Chi in the decorous seclusion of the Gardens, they cross the Ring Road into the rumbustious expanses of the Park.

Hyde Park is where the libido runs free: generations of lovers have pined and lusted in its shade, carving their initials on the bark of its trees and the weathered timber of its benches, but never did it thrill to so much depravity as in the brief lull before the Battle of Waterloo. It was the summer of 1814: Napoleon was beaten, or so Europe thought. Knightsbridge Woman, clad in the Empire Line, gave a collective sigh of relief. Dresses could be imported once more from Paris, where the great Leroy, tailor to Madame Recamier and Empress Josephine, was plugging low-necked muslins over flesh-coloured vests. (They were a good deal easier to wear than the gowns Madame Recamier had brought over in 1802 when, during a pause in hostilities, she had shocked all London by walking in Kensington Gardens dressed like a Greek statue, with the draperies clinging to her form.) 'Naked fashions,' Jane Austen tartly observed. Nevertheless with a few modifications the classical style caught on.

Lord Byron meanwhile composed *The Waltz*, a poem about the wicked new dance in which gentlemen clasped their partners' *uncorseted* waists. The duennas complained it was encitement to lechery and, adding to the Season's frissons, the Duke of Wellington arrived back from the front with his officers, some of whom were awfully handsome and all of whom were frightfully brave. The London ladies swooned in droves. White's Club laid on a ball for two thousand people, while the Battle of Trafalgar was re-staged on the Serpentine with the French ships in flames, sinking to the strains of 'God Save the King.'

'Naked fashions,' Jane Austen tartly observed.

[31]

Outside the Park, where ropes would not become tangled with the trees, Balloon Ascents drew such crowds that spectator tickets had to be issued at half a guinea each. The Hyde Park Fair was meant to last a fortnight. It was intended to be an expression of the Nation's joyfulness that the Almighty had seen fit to deliver Britain from Napoleon's great scheme for a united Europe, but such was the rioting and drunkenness that Lord Sidmouth, the Secretary of State for Home Affairs, tried to close the Fair down. The stall-holders objected, and the London pawnbrokers trebled their business as the intoxicated public raised funds to buy more drink.

'Never within the memory of Man', thundered the *Morning Post*, 'have there been witnessed such scenes of drunkenness and dissipation. Clothes, furniture, and worst of all *tools* were pawned for the sake of momentary enjoyment.'

Just as the excitement died down Napoleon escaped from Elba, marched across France and entered Paris to begin the Hundred Days which were to end with the Battle of Waterloo. It was decided to celebrate the British victories with two gigantic statues of Lord Nelson and the Duke of Wellington. The Treasury set aside £310,000 for the purpose. Nelson soared to the skies but by 1817, two years after Waterloo, the statue of the Duke had still not been erected. There was a taboo in force against commemorative sculpture of heroes who were not yet dead. The patriotic society known as the Ladies of England took matters into their own hands. They commissioned Sir Richard Westmacott to make a gigantic

[32]

replica of a Roman horse. Having lived in Rome, the sculptor knew they had got their symbolism wrong.

He deftly modelled a colossal figure from the Roman group the Ladies had chosen, but of a man not a horse. Loosely named 'Achilles' the hero was stark naked, according to the best traditions of Greece and Rome. He was erected in 1822 at the south-west corner of Hyde Park. The Ladies of England were horrified and demanded that a fig leaf be applied at once. There were questions in parliament. The Duke, who was known as a 'ladies' man', stayed stoically silent.

8

Village Life

L ONDONERS LOVE TO LIVE in villages. Each village acquires its own cachet, but as the villages have all run into each other only the locals know where they begin and end. Visitors to our historic metropolis are often surprised to find it riddled with invisible boundaries which it is social death to ignore.

Take the fine line dividing Knightsbridge from Belgravia. Baffled foreign leaseholders cannot understand why the English make such a fuss about it, when *rational* people don't even know it exists. Estate agents are more sensitive. To make a slip in the postcode could cost a mega buck, and most have grasped that while Knightsbridge grew up higgledy-piggledy to house the Service Industries, Belgravia was purpose built for the Seriously Rich.

Within living memory Cobb, the Butcher, stood at the corner of Basil Street serving as a focal point for both villages. It was a proper, old-fashioned butcher's with sawdust on the floor, and a cashier who sat behind a little window ringing up the takings in an ornate, bronze till. 'Cobb's' – the 's' is invisible, but it is always pronounced – had been there since 1802, forty-seven years longer than Harrods. It kept open through two world wars, and employed a fleet of bike boys who delivered all over London. The most sought-after job was taking the rations to Buckingham Palace, where amidst the wartime austerity the King and Queen followed the high moral tone set by Queen Mary. As Empress of India she had sported the finest diamonds in the world, but during the War she successfully popularised scrag end of mutton. Queen Mary was a stickler for abiding by the meat ration, believing it was a sure way to beat the Germans.

She jibbed, however, at other forms of economy. When evacuated to Badminton she took her entire staff of sixty-three, causing acute concern to her niece, the Duchess of Beaufort, who looked out of the window to see the immense convoy advancing up the drive.

Many of the older inhabitants feel Knightsbridge stopped being a *proper* village when Cobb's moved from Basil Street to new premises off Sloane Square. It was the era of the Sloane Rangers. East Chelsea was enjoying a boom and the Cordon Blues were out in force, wielding their Sabatier knives as taught by Prue Leith and Tante Marie. Anxious to retain their provenance, Cobb's put 'of Knightsbridge' above the shop front, even when ignominiously re-situated opposite the bric-à-brac department of Peter Jones.

In Knightsbridge itself they were supplanted by a tobacconist and the lamenting was universal.

'Dunhill,' snorted one grand lady. 'Why don't they go back to Bond Street, where they belong?'

French by birth, she is residentially a *Belgravian* to the back teeth, but she has sold clothes in *Knightsbridge* for longer than anyone dares remember. Crowned heads fight for bargains at her sales, and crested Rolls-Royces arrive to carry away the spoils. Her prejudice against the tobacconist has nothing to do with the dangers of smoking. The Chairman of Dunhill, the Marquis of Douro, a former Member of the European Parliament, is heir to the Duke of Wellington, whose town house, No. 1 Piccadilly, is in *Mayfair.*

Rich Americans, oil tycoons and corporate bankers, who *rent* a great deal of property in both Knightsbridge and Belgravia, are mystified by these parochial distinctions. Having no sense of History, it is a bit of an eye-opener for them to learn that the heart of Knightsbridge village was originally the nasty triangle between the Royal Bank of Scotland and the Sloane Street traffic lights, where cars and buses stand permanently gridlocked. Here in Samuel Pepys's day there was a village green, a bona fide maypole, a duck pond and some stocks. As the spot was notorious for highwaymen, the stocks survived until the time of the Battle of Trafalgar.

In the 1660s the rustic hamlet lay so far outside the City Walls that it became a burial ground for plague victims. Some say their bones lie under Knightsbridge Green itself; some say under 'the hump', the promontory opposite Harrods crowned by the smart new headquarters of Sanderson, the wallpaper people. The point could only be proved by digging up Montpelier Street or the Royal Bank of Scotland. Unfortunately the information about the bones leaked into a number of guide books. To appease English Heritage, Westminster Council stuck up a blue sign marked 'Knightsbridge Green'. They put it opposite Park Close, just beyond the cluster of bus stops on the

Scotch House side. There is not a blade of grass in sight, so it has done little to stem the flood of enquiries from puzzled tourists. Globe-trotting Australians tend to get lost there when searching for the Grove Tavern, Beauchamp Place, site of the first cricket match between England and Australia.

To confuse things even more, in modern Estate-Agent-Speak 'Knightsbridge Village' now refers exclusively to the cobbled streets and jasmine-wreathed mews houses tucked behind Rutland Gate. It boasts four second-hand dress shops, two wine bars, three pubs, abundant charm, a safe deposit and a picturesque view of the Brompton Oratory. There is no butcher, baker or candlestick-maker, though 48 Cheval Place has pretensions with 'The Old Bakery' scrawled in Gothic script on the front door.

Full of converted gas lamps and hitching-posts, the narrow lanes were never expected to become the smart part of Knightsbridge. The modest terraces sprang up in the 1820s to house tradespeople. No one above the rank of Esquire lived in Montpelier Square and in the neighbouring alleyways at least two persons are listed in the Post Office Directory of 1859 as 'cowkeeper'. But with the military on the doorstep since the time of George II, the Service Industries *thrived*.

Harriette Wilson, the courtesan who drew from the Duke of Wellington the celebrated reply, 'Publish and be damned,' when she tried to blackmail him over her *Memoirs*, lived at 16 Trevor Square. Her book sent frissons through Georgian London. Harriette changed her lovers as easily as her shoes. The Duke of Argyll, Lord Ponsonby, Lord Byron and even the young Lord Melbourne were among her victims. The book went into thirty-one editions. She published the first from Paris, but the London version appeared in serial form. At 2pm on publication days her publisher's office in the Haymarket was besieged by impatient crowds waiting for the latest chapter. Harriette blackmailed at the rate of £200 a head, taking hard cash from those who wanted their names kept *out* of the book. After making a profit of £10,000 she bought the corner house in Trevor Square, where she started to write a second book, *Clara Gazul*.

During the War there were two brothels in Knightsbridge; one in Basil Street, which had been taken over by the Americans, and a more genteel establishment in Cheval Place, which catered for the Royal Canadian Air Force. The Basil Street brothel was notorious. Everyone recalls that it was *there*, but no one can remember the address. The Hans Crescent Hotel had been requisitioned for our allies, and stories abound of drunken GIs carried back to their quarters and hoisted to bed on dumb waiters. Mention the Basil Street brothel, however, and informants grow strangely coy.

Smith and McCartney, an enterprising pair of lady carpet-fitters, were called in to refurbish some flats in Basil Mansions after the bomb damage. One day they discovered a five-pound note beneath the underfelt at premises owned by a 'respectable little old lady in black'.

'Oh, keep it,' she said. But when they tore up more carpet they found the whole room was lined with fivers. At this the old lady flew into a violent rage, cursing the girl who had rented the place in the Blitz. 'Overcharging

[38]

the poor boys,' she screamed. Even Smith and McCartney cannot recall the address.

Mrs McGrath is less reticent. A legend in her time, she bought No. 8 Cheval Place in 1952 and transformed it into The Dress Box, the smartest second-hand clothes shop in London. It has remained so for several decades.

'Lots of the cottages housed call-girls,' she says. 'You could always tell the professionals. They stood on the street corners, trailing their fox furs and trying to look like Marlene Dietrich in *The Blue Angel*. When we took over No. 8, the cellars were full of photographs left behind by the Canadians. Action shots. We were riveted. In those days there was a Film Censor, so we'd never seen anything like it.'

Patriotic services were also on offer in Thurloe Square. Captain Oliver Cox of the 18th King Edward's Own Cavalry remembers arriving in London in 1945. He had sprained his ankle in Cheltenham and was limping about Knightsbridge, bandaged like a War Hero. Stunningly handsome, and later to star in a film as the young Rupert Brooke, he rescued two girls from a bunch of carousing Americans.

'I was on leave from India and looking for a bed. The girls were so grateful. They took me to their digs in Thurloe Square. Their landlady was the West Indian wife of a British Army Major. She saw it as part of the War Effort to keep the troops happy. The drawing-room had a grand piano and the tarts were £2 a night.'

For his gallantry he was offered the blonde in black satin sheets, the showpiece of the house, for free.

'She wore parachute silk camiknickers which peeled

upwards like a banana,' he remembers nostalgically. 'I thought it was love, but next morning she said, "Well, dear, don't you think it's time you got out?" There was breakfast in the basement with bread, butter, bacon and egg, tea and *fresh* milk. It was astonishing. Milk came mostly dried and bacon was still on ration.'

After the War many of the cottages which had withstood the bombing were let to Harrods' doormen, who were recruited from the Foot Guards. Nobody coveted such poky accommodation and, even today, Knightsbridge Woman of an older, more indomitable breed might refuse to live south of Rutland Gate on the grounds that anything with 'mews' in the address is 'ostlers' quarters'.

'There is New Money; there is Old Money; and there is Very Old Money,' said one estate agent cautiously. 'You can usually tell which you are handling, if you offer something marginal, explaining that it's *really* Belgravia. Many people nowadays *prefer* Knightsbridge. They think it's more villagey, more cottagey and, dare I say it, more *English*. I don't think it matters any more that the houses were built for artisans, though of course some people feel safer with white stucco.'

9

Marriage à la Mode

ROYAL PATRONAGE of the clean air from the time of William and Mary gave Kensington the reputation of a health spa. Knightsbridge shared in the glory. The western part of the hamlet stood on a slight hill, commanding fine views of the surrounding countryside. The Duke of Kingston built a splendid house, No. 3 Knightsbridge, on the high ground, believing the pure air would be good for his horses.

He had done very well out of the Battle of Culloden with a troop called Kingston's Light Horse. His stud groom, Richard Tattersall, obtained a ninety-nine-year lease on land near Hyde Park Corner, where he established Tattersall's, the home of British bloodstock sales. The nearby Turf Tavern was the first headquarters of the Jockey Club. On viewing days the rich and fashionable flocked to Tattersall's and when the lease expired in 1864 the famous horse mart moved to Knightsbridge Green, where it occupied two acres of stabling until the end of the last War.

Tattersall began his bloodstock enterprise during the Duke's lifetime. After his master's death in 1773, he disposed of the Kingston stud and was about to pay the

profits to the Duke's colourful widow, Elizabeth Chudleigh, when he was stopped by a court injunction. One
of the great beauties of her day, Miss Chudleigh was left
badly provided for by her father's death. She retired to
the country at the tender age of six, but by good luck
had a love affair at fifteen with William Pulteney, the
future Earl of Bath, whom she met when he was out
shooting. Sporting events had an invigorating effect on
Miss Chudleigh. She was soon back in London, as a Maid
of Honour to the Princess Augusta. She had set her heart
on marrying a Duke.

The first one, the 6th Duke of Hamilton, got away. He
wrote passionate letters to Elizabeth, which were inter-
cepted by her aunt, and eventually he married a Miss
Gunning. At Winchester Races, however, the jilted
Miss Chudleigh fell in love with the Hon. Augustus
Hervey, a grandson of the Earl of Bristol. They married
in secret, Elizabeth keeping her maiden name for fear of
losing her place at Court.

She had a reputation for fast behaviour and shocked
Horace Walpole by appearing at a fancy dress ball clad
as Iphigenia, but 'so naked you would have taken her for
Andromeda' (the bare-breasted heroine whom Perseus
found damply chained to a rock). When Hervey, who was
a lieutenant in the Navy, returned from the West Indies
the couple did not get on, but as the failing health of the
Earl of Bristol meant her husband might succeed to
the title, Elizabeth confessed her marriage to the Princess
Augusta. Made *Dowager* Princess by the early demise of
'Poor Fred', Augusta had grown status-conscious. She
briskly advised the presumptive Countess to get her

[42]

marriage registered, and to check the paperwork. At this point Miss Chudleigh, who was forty, became mistress to the Duke of Kingston. He was extremely rich and in 1760 Elizabeth gave a birthday ball for the Prince of Wales. Her parties immediately became the most fashionable in London.

Having found the perfect Duke, Elizabeth wanted to marry him, but could not face the scandal of divorce from a husband whom nobody knew she had wed. A consistory court eventually declared her a spinster, though, it later transpired, without legally dissolving the first union. She married Kingston and set about embellishing No. 3 Knightsbridge in earnest. The combination of the free-spending Duchess and the incomparable horses made the spot so famous that 'Kingston Hill' stuck as a nickname to that part of Knightsbridge long after the high ground had been flattened out of existence.

When the Duke died, he left his whole estate to Elizabeth on condition she remained a widow. She sailed for Italy, visited the Pope, and delighted all Rome by having her yacht brought up the Tiber. In the meantime Kingston's nephew contested the will, accusing the widowed Duchess of bigamy. When she tried to return to England her Roman banker, who had got wind of the scandal, made difficulties about money. Elizabeth went down to his office with a loaded pistol and threatened to blow out his brains.

Hervey was by now Earl of Bristol and a bigamy case was brought against his Countess in the Court of King's Bench. Keen to hang onto her title and estate, the Duchess pulled rank. She demanded to be tried by her peers in the High Court of Parliament. It was not often convened for such a purpose, so the first day's proceedings were entirely taken up by the peers going in procession from the House of Lords to Westminster Hall in company with the judges, Garter King of Arms and a train of people attending on the Earl of Bathurst, who was Lord High Steward. The hearing lasted for seven days. Unanimously declared guilty (though the Duke of Newcastle murmured, 'Unintentionally,' as sentence was pronounced) Elizabeth narrowly escaped the common punishment for bigamy, which was to be branded on the hand with red hot irons. She claimed exemption by right of her peerage as *Countess of Bristol*, a privilege vigorously contested by the Attorney General.

The demoted Duchess sailed for France. Eventually she settled in Russia, where she became a friend of Catherine the Great. She purchased an estate near St Petersburg upon which she set up a brandy factory. Severing all connection with Knightsbridge, she named it 'Chudleigh' after the Devon village, famed for the manufacture of coarse woollen cloth.

10

Power Dressing

ONE OF THE present writer's cherished memories is of employing the unemployable young to paint a kitchen. This was not in the job-hungry nineties but in the early eighties, before the recession got properly under way. Terracotta was the theme, and the overall effect was to be 'rus in urbe' with festoons of dried herbs strung from every rafter, for the Cook (Knightsbridge Man by day, but a *bon viveur* in exotic South Chelsea by night) to clip and sniff as the spirit took him.

The painters, fresh from art college, were heavily into New Romanticism. They were anxious that the client should take a Mistress so that they could fill his king-size bed with little cushions, covered in lawn and handkerchief lace, of which they were the sole purveyors. The commission, however, was matt emulsion in straight terracotta, a difficult hue with a well-known tendency to turn salmon pink on drying, or chocolate brown when not lit by the afternoon sun. Both painters were ladies of impeccable upbringing and born within that blissful era of interior decoration when the client was still allowed to be *right*.

They went to endless trouble over the terracotta,

reducing their fee and popping in at all hours to see what shade the latest coat had dried. One morning they distinguished themselves by arriving after they had been to an all-night party, slipping into their overalls and setting to work before the sun was up. The client's slumbers were disturbed by a sudden howl of reproach. Fearing salmon pink had once again blushed through, he dashed into the kitchen to find the bossier of the two standing at the foot of the ladder, upbraiding her mate, 'Oh, Julia, you've been painting in your pearls again!'

Pearls are an integral part of the English Way of Dressing. Even with the dowdiest outfit they reek of aristocratic breeding, a snobbery dating back to when Charles I banned imitation jewellery at Court to protect the British oyster fisheries. Since then pearls have been considered the correct rig for every occasion. You can wear them to parties. You can wear them to polo. You can wear them to Cowes where, even with a bikini, they fulfil that strictest of naval requirements 'dressed over all'. The only time in English history that pearls have been frowned upon was the era of the Charleston, when long strings dangling down from the flattened bosoms of the lady dancers would sometimes loop themselves dangerously round a partner's feet.

It can take ten years for an oyster to make a pearl. Natural pearls cost the earth. You can find a few at Cartier in Sloane Street, but most Knightsbridge jewellers rely on *cultured* pearls, which are not to be confused with vulgar imitations. Cultured pearls come from *real* oysters, which have been artificially interfered with – usually in

[46]

'Oh, Julia, you've been painting in your pearls again!'

Japan. They are therefore *real* pearls and still of great price.

Ever since the notorious Australian gang raided Lady Astor's shop in the sixties, Knightsbridge retailers have been nervous of too much outward show. The good stuff is often removed from the windows at half-past five, and replicas are laid out to deter burglars. Ciro puts up discreet brass plates marked 'Night Display'. Kutchinsky, further along the Brompton Road, sweeps the windows clean each evening.

Originally pearls were not a means of Power Dressing, but symbols of purity. As a teenager Elizabeth I wore two strings in imitation of her wronged mother, Anne Boleyn. This emphasised her famous virginity. Lettice Knollys, her cousin and rival in love, flaunted *four* strings from neck to navel. She married the Earl of Leicester who, fearing the two women would be at each other's throats after his death, sat up all night on a Dutch battlefield trying to make a will, dividing his goods between them. The English lost the battle, but Elizabeth got the pearls. She wore them in *six* strands neck to navel ever afterwards.

Queen Mary, our present Queen's grandmother, perfected the art of wearing pearls to impress. As Empress of India she owned rather more of them than most people. She adored shopping in Knightsbridge, but she was no slave to fashion. After the War she would often poke about Harrods in a frock that was nearly twenty years out of date. She had inherited certain lavish tastes, however, from her father, Prince Francis of Teck, who was a fastidious interior decorator. On the great State occasions of her life – her Coronation, the Investiture of the Prince

[48]

of Wales and the Delhi Durbar – Queen Mary stole the show. She did not wear strings of pearls. She wore *swags* of them. They must have given her orthopaedic support for, while her head bore the weight of a blazing tiara, her neck would often be, quite literally, *stiff* with pearls.

Although French women tend to sneer at the English Way of Dressing, they covet our twin-sets and envy our pearls, handed down from mother to daughter according to the laws of primogeniture. When Charles II took a French mistress, Louise de Keroualle, he created her Duchess of Portsmouth. This was shortly after he had provided for Nell Gwyn at No. 79 Pall Mall. He firmly installed Louise at Kensington House, a good two miles out of London and out of range of Nell's malice. This didn't prevent some picturesque slanging matches.

When the London mob stoned a closed coach, believing it carried the unpopular Louise, Nell Gwyn stuck her head out of the window, shouting, 'Stop, you fools. I am the *Protestant* whore, not the Catholic one!'

Fierce rivalry ensued. In a studied piece of Power Undressing, Louise had herself painted in one pearl earring and a negligée which revealed her peerless left nipple. The fashion did not catch on, but Nell had herself painted by Sir Peter Lely, tastefully nude in a pastoral setting. Louise, who would stop at nothing, arranged a French divertissement called 'le sandwich'. She and two other Court ladies dressed as the three Graces, and disrobed before the King *toutes ensembles*. He had them *en suite*.

In another picture of Louise, now in the National Portrait Gallery, the bold woman has carelessly wound her pearls round the neck of her black page boy. The child leans against her knee, offering her a branch of coral and a shell full of pearls, which the Duchess appears to disdain. Curious to know why, I contacted one of her descendants, a Knightsbridge lady of otherwise impeccable pedigree.

'Did Charles give her the pearls?' I asked.

Quick as a flash came the reply, 'No, but he gave her Goodwood.'

She was nearly right. Louise's *son*, Charles Lennox, Duke of Richmond, bought Goodwood as a hunting lodge, but the King did give Louise a string of pearls valued at £4000. This was to console her after he passed on a nasty dose of syphilis, which he had caught from one of his other mistresses. The Duchess went to Tunbridge Wells to recover, but she immediately fell foul of the Marchioness of Worcester, who preceded her through a door. Louise remonstrated. With the devastating candour of English matronhood, Lady Worcester told her that titles gained by prostitution did not count. The nettled Duchess wrote to the King, who soothed her nerves by sending an entire detachment of the Household Brigade to escort her back to Kensington.

11

Kensington Gore

L EAFY LANES and market gardens still stretched
from Brompton to Fulham in the early part of the
nineteenth century, while woods and pastures bor-
dered the route from Kensington to Westminster. The
Hyde Park Turnpike was supposed to pay for the upkeep
of the roads, but Kensington Gore (from 'gara', the Anglo-
Saxon word for unploughed land) lived up to its name,
being the place where carriages came unstuck and axles
jammed in the mud.

Gore House stood back from the road, an isolated
country property, serene and friendly amid walnut trees
and mulberry walks. It had overlooked Hyde Park since
1750, and would have continued to do so had those royal
vandals, Victoria and Albert, not got hold of the site
after the Great Exhibition, and had the pretty building
knocked down to make way for the Albert Hall. A mile
of pasture land separated Gore House from London. It
was also surrounded by a walled garden offering privacy
and seclusion. In 1808 William Wilberforce, exhausted
from pushing his bill for the Abolition of Slavery through
Parliament, took it on a long lease, hoping to restore his
health. (It had been impaired by too much commuting.)

Like most MPs of his time Wilberforce kept up two establishments, one at Clapham where his family lived, and one in Palace Yard near the Houses of Parliament.

'I shall save five or six hundred a year,' he wrote optimistically, regarding the move to Knightsbridge as a sound piece of domestic economy. Wilberforce had forgotten that by abolishing slavery he had already become a famous man.

The Great Reformer spent the early hours of the day in private and family prayer. After that he was obliged to dispense extensive hospitality. A throng of visitors began arriving at breakfast-time and continued through the day. Wilberforce soon found that living nearer London afforded him not more time for parliamentary business, but less. The gardens of Gore House were an earthly Paradise, full of lilacs and laburnums, where swallows twittered and nightingales sang. To visit Mr Wilberforce became a pleasure as well as the fashion, but his domestic expenditure doubled, as those repelled by the thought of trekking to far-distant Clapham eagerly sought him out.

Worse still, the great man was patron of sixty-nine different charities, so that Kensington Gore soon became a clearing house for British Philanthropy, as well as a centre for fervent evangelism. Lord Erskine might dismount during an early ride through the Park for a chat about cruelty to animals. Royal Dukes dropped in without a word of warning, particularly the Duke of Kent, who lived only half a mile away at Knightsbridge House, or the Duke of Gloucester, who wanted to see more Bibles distributed among the heathen. Even that notable old gossip, Madame de Staël, called, pronouncing Wilberforce not only the most religious man in England, but also the wittiest.

It was a great worry for Mrs Wilberforce. Poor Barbara was not cut out to be Knightsbridge Woman. Her two preoccupations in life were health and hellfire: the promotion of the one in this world and the avoidance of the other in the next. Not the most soignée of hostesses, she made little domestic economies – wholly in keeping with the rustic simplicities of the Gore, perhaps, but lacking in tact towards the smart new neighbours. Wilberforce, at one of his own breakfasts, found himself sitting next to a Church of England Bishop so unimpressed by the frugal fare that he *roared* for more bread and butter.

Another of Barbara's worries was the company they kept. Madame de Stael had been the mistress of Talleyrand, while the Duke of Kent (before he married Queen Victoria's mother) lived with a French Canadian lady, Madame de St Laurent. That he had been faithful to her for twenty-seven happy years, only renouncing her from a sense of duty when the death of the heiress to the throne, Princess Charlotte, brought about the Succession Crisis, made no difference. In Barbara's eyes she was a sure passport to hellfire. On top of this Mrs Hannah More, one of the great Evangelicals of the day, had reproved Wilberforce for pretending to be out when the crush of visitors proved unmanageable. It was tantamount, she said, to encouraging the servants to tell *lies*.

Hannah More had been a friend of the Wilberforces from the earliest days of their marriage. She was celebrated as one of the 'Nine Living Muses of Great Britain'. She had written to the King to complain of Sunday routs and assemblies, because fashionable ladies could not attend them without having their hair done beforehand. This caused hairdressers and ladies' maids to miss Church.

Elizabeth Fry, the reformer of women's prisons, was another visitor to Gore House. In her Quaker garb, with covered bosom and high collar, she suited Barbara's requirements a good deal better than the *demi-monde*, dressed still in the naked fashions censured by Jane Austen. When the ladies withdrew after dinner, leaving the men to their port, interesting facts respecting convicts were discussed at Wilberforce's table, including 'damage done to boys cooped up with lusty men'. As Leigh Hunt acidly remarked, Wilberforce contrived to combine 'the most terrific ideas of the Next World with the most comfortable enjoyment of this'.

In the end the Great Reformer had to withdraw from 'the gay and irreligious society' of the Gore. The Wilberforces moved to Battersea Rise. It was a pity they never got to know Madame de St Laurent better. In the best tradition of French royal mistresses she ended her life as a nun, and as the Duke of Kent wrote to his friend Mr Greevey, 'She comes of a very good family and has never been an actress.'

12

Great Debtors

N o NOTIONS of Political Correctness troubled the next occupant of Gore House. The Countess of Blessington was born in Co. Tipperary, the daughter of a dissolute Irish magistrate. He went by the name of Beau Power, or Shiver the Frills, as he always wore top boots and a white cravat among the local squirearchy. For a time he turned newspaper tycoon, publishing the *Munster Mercury*. He swiftly lost a fortune and engaged his daughter, Marguerite, when she was fourteen, to a mentally unstable Captain of Dragoons. This drunken brute beat her so viciously that she ran away to Dublin.

By the time she was eighteen she was living in London, a recognised beauty, painted by Sir Thomas Lawrence. His portrait of her in white satin, with a posy of roses and forget-me-nots tucked into her exquisite bosom, hangs in the Wallace Collection. Her husband, Captain St Leger Farmer, died in 1817 after falling from the window of the King's Bench Prison in a drunken stupor. The following year she married Viscount Mountjoy, later the first Earl of Blessington. The Earl drew £30,000 a year (roughly twice the income of a Royal Duke) from his Irish estates, and in 1822 the couple set off on a continental holiday which was to last for the next seven years.

Lord Blessington was the most generous and amiable of men. The Countess's sister, Mary Anne Power, and Alfred Count D'Orsay, the handsomest man of his time, accompanied the expedition. The Earl, whose ten-year-old son had died, took such a liking to D'Orsay that he decided to settle his fortune on him by marrying him to his daughter, Lady Harriet Gardiner. Still mourning for her brother, the unfortunate schoolgirl was shipped out to Naples, where she took an instant dislike to D'Orsay, though of course she married him in accordance with her father's wishes.

Harriet swiftly paled into insignificance beside her radiant stepmother, but the D'Orsays remained with the Blessingtons, who travelled through Italy leasing palazzos, visiting the exiled Lord Byron and generally creating waves of good fellowship wherever they went. The idyll was cut short when the Earl died suddenly of an apoplexy, leaving Lady Blessington with a jointure of only £2000 a year. She returned to London, let her house in Seamore Place and took Gore House, where for the next thirteen years she presided as one of London's most dazzling hostesses. Harriet returned to Ireland to live with her grandmother, old Lady Mountjoy, who was vigorously contesting the Earl's will. D'Orsay took a house in the Gore and devoted the rest of his life to consoling Lady Blessington.

To augment her income Marguerite turned to journalism. *Conversations with Lord Byron* had already made her literary reputation. She quickly became editress of the

Book of Beauty, writing also for *The Keepsake* and the *Daily News*, which was briefly edited by Charles Dickens. Lady Blessington was engaged at the then phenomenal rate of £500 a year. The forerunner of many Knightsbridge lady writers, she dashed off popular novels in her spare time. For the next twenty years it was estimated that her income from journalism was £3000 a year. Alas, expenditure at Gore House ran at £4000 a year.

The Gore House coterie included eminent politicians and nearly all the leading literary men of the day. This greatly annoyed Lady Holland and Lady Jersey, rival hostesses always on the lookout for new scandals to bring down Lady Blessington, but she was virtuous as well as being successful. The beautiful Irish Countess had a whole battery of admirers. Dickens, Disraeli, Bulwer Lytton, Walter Savage Landor, the Duke of Wellington and even Prince Louis Napoleon, the future President of the French Republic, paid court to 'the most gorgeous Lady Blessington'.

After one of those political upheavals which were constantly troubling the volatile French, Prince Louis even came to live at Gore House, having just escaped from prison disguised as a workman with a plank over his shoulders. Lady Blessington asked the Archbishop of Canterbury to drop in to meet her royal protégé. He came, to the mortification of Lady Holland and Lady Jersey.

Mrs Wilberforce's economies had left the interior of the mansion in a sorry state, but Lady Blessington soon restored that lavish style to which she had grown accustomed when her husband was alive. The most famous room was her library. Its shelves were edged with white enamel, with mirrors in the interstices, cleverly reflecting the light from the sumptuous chandeliers. The apple-green curtains were of silk damask, and the chaises-longues and the white and gold chairs were upholstered to match. Here Lady Blessington lived with an Italian greyhound, and a white poodle with amber eyes which was painted by Landseer. She also kept a mynah bird, trained to say 'Up Guards and at 'em!' to the great delight of the Duke of Wellington, who had used the phrase with such effect at the Battle of Waterloo. The Countess was a friend to all who were in need and, despite the claims of seven or eight dependants from her own family, she had no real problems – except for D'Orsay.

Everyone loved Alfred D'Orsay. All who met him fell under his spell. He was the greatest dandy of his time. His brilliant wit and elegant dress were the talk of the Town. His clothes were so famous that his tailors would withhold their bills for fear of losing his patronage. He was a brilliant painter. Wellington was so pleased with one likeness that he said, 'At last I have been painted like a gentleman. I'll never sit to anyone else.'

Having come by the Earl's fortune so pleasantly, however, D'Orsay never quite grasped that one day it would run out. It was said that when his tailors heard he was in difficulties they would line the pockets of his coats with banknotes, so that he should not feel uncomfortable.

Like Lady Blessington, he was generous to a fault. When he met a Major in the Guards who was talking of selling his commission to pay some debts, D'Orsay found the idea so extraordinary that he asked the man to lend him £10. Reluctantly the Major complied. The following day D'Orsay called on him and gave him £750.

'I staked your £10 at Crockford's,' he said simply.

No one could run up debts like D'Orsay. Even Queen Victoria's father, the profligate Duke of Kent, whose creditors were still presenting accounts seventeen years after his death, had not spent money so fast. In the interim, between the Earl of Blessington's death and the arrival of the annuities on his estates, the extravagant Count had collected £103,500 worth of bills. Anxious to save Lady Blessington embarrassment D'Orsay tried to go bankrupt, but as he was neither a businessman nor a landowner he found he did not qualify.

One day, as he was walking through London, a heavy hand was laid on his shoulder. He was arrested for an unpaid bill of £300 to his bootmaker, M. Henry of Paris. Terrified at every step that a bailiff might come upon him, he moved into Gore House where he could live in safety, taking exercise in the spacious grounds without venturing into the streets. Even this did not prevent him from *shopping*. The tradesmen came to the door. The Count was as elegant as ever, ordering gloves from abroad in a dead leaf colour, but he only went out after sundown or on Sundays, when the bailiffs could not strike.

Eventually a bailiff, disguised as a pastry cook, gained entry. By a sustained display of the art of dressing, D'Orsay kept him waiting until nightfall. When he was finally attired to meet the fellow he could not be arrested for another thirty-six hours, for the next day was Sunday, so the Count remained inviolable until Monday morning.

Slowly but surely the creditors closed in. With his valet

and one portmanteau D'Orsay fled to Paris. Two weeks later Lady Blessington followed him. Gore House was put up for auction with all its fine fixtures and fittings. The day before the sale Lady Jersey headed a contingent of ladies who had come to scrutinise the contents. The sale realised £12,000, enough to pay Lady Blessington's debts. She took an apartment in Paris, and the literary fraternity of the Gore was gone for ever. Thackeray wept.

13

Nannies and Horses

'HYDE PARK! HOW an old Nanny, as Englishmen once did to Agincourt, thrills still to the mention of that name. For many the richest moments of their lives passed there. Nannies were going to it before the First World War . . .' But, as Jonathan Gathorne-Hardy explains in *The Rise and Fall of the British Nanny*, it was in the twenties and thirties that it peaked. Those decades saw great technical improvements in the pram.

Mornings might be spent in the nursery or garden squares. In the afternoon, rain or shine, the nannies made for the Park, pushing their younger charges in sturdy coach-built four-wheelers, lacquered maroon or navy blue. In winter they wore cloche hats, long coats and sensible shoes. In summer the beige of the Norland uniforms mingled with the rich browns of the Princess Christian nurses, offset by the cornflower blue with-obligatory starched-cap of the Chiltern girls.

'What a sight, a vast concourse of nannies, thronging, drifting, sitting, rocking, more numerous than the buffalo on the plain, more talkative than starlings at a moot,' remembers Gathorne-Hardy, and as if drawn by some unseen magnetic force they would foregather on the gravel walks either side of Rotten Row to look with unfeigned delight at the horses cantering down the smartest bridle path in the whole world.

There were, and still are, Nanny zones in the Park. The best known anecdote in *The Rise and Fall* took place on a bench behind the Albert Memorial, where one sunny afternoon in the sixties the nanny to David Pryce-Jones's children took her seat. She was joined by a veteran nanny, wheeling a pram with a discreet gold coronet painted on the gleaming coachwork.

'Is your Mummy a titled Mummy?' asked the older woman, eyeing the Pryce-Jones Nanny suspiciously, and on learning she was not, delivered the immortal rebuke, 'This bench is for titled Mummies' Nannies only, Nanny!'

Another favourite spot was the Daisy Walk at the east end of the Serpentine. The approach was through Albert Gate, where bronze stags stand rampant on the gate-posts. Live sheep grazed Hyde Park until the 1930s. Feeding the birds and picking the daisies were among the innocent pleasures allowed. Serious misbehaviour was rare. Nasty little boys got smacked and were taken home yelling and kicking, while little girls looked on disapprovingly.

Beatings were administered by fathers. The Mitford girls* briefly encountered a character called the Unkind Nanny, who thumped Nancy's head against a bed post. Nancy claimed not to remember the incident, though she vividly recalled the sacking of the Unkind Nanny. 'Fa', Lord Redesdale, entered the nursery himself. 'There was

---

*For a time they lived at 47 Rutland Gate.

'This bench is for titled Mummies' Nannies only, Nanny!'

a confrontation,' she wrote later, 'as of two mastodons.' Nancy's sympathies were with the Nanny.

Nannies had to be physically strong. Horrid two-year-olds often found themselves hoisted aloft and strapped aft, aboard a Silver Cross pram, their feet dangling in the 'well', which was a feature of the larger models. Harrods still stock Silver Cross bassinets in the traditional navy blue, or in a rather *nouveau* white with a navy hood. They are eagerly bought by Americans, who want something 'typically English'. (True Brits, of course, go more for pushchairs, which fold into the back of a Range Rover, load easily onto the No. 9 bus or get shoved into Nanny's mini.) Coach-built in Leeds, the modern Silver Cross retails *from* £500. 'Silver Stream' and 'Marlborough' – the very names reek of privilege – are the popular models. Light and easy to wheel they may be, but as symbols of a lifestyle they are not a patch on the old, sturdy prams with their chrome side-pieces, curving up to support real ivory handles, fixed between shining hexagonal nuts. The Nannies steered them like battle tanks, their umbrellas hooked over the handle.

Working-class children coveted the wheels of a Silver Cross pram to make Dilly carts, simple imitations of their fathers' coster barrows. They used them to collect bits of scrap metal, as playthings, or to pull along younger brothers and sisters. *Nice* children envied them wildly. Toddler seats upon which extra children could be piled indiscriminately, while baby lay supine beneath, came into general use after the War, when extra nursery maids were becoming expensive. In the 1970s blue-uniformed nannies from the Walton Day Nursery still crossed the road by the Cavalry Barracks every morning, pushing prams loaded with two-year-olds. The traffic always stopped, but toddler seats are now banned because of stringent new safety laws.

Most families don't insist on nannies wearing uniform any more. Harrods supply the Norland uniform, but usually to students. They are expected to wear it throughout the two-year NNEB course, but after that reaction sets in.

'If I were asked to wear my uniform in London,' said a trained Norlander passionately, 'I would turn down the job.'

Princess Christian, the grandest of the three top training centres, was founded by Queen Victoria's fifth child, Princess Helena, later Princess Christian of Schleswig-Holstein, as part of the Gentlewoman's Help Society. They reckon their uniform still has plenty of cachet, and report an increased demand for nannies dressed in it. Their headquarters are in Manchester, so it is just possible that clients are recommended by rather formal Scottish Duchesses. Jeans and sweatshirts are considered perfectly acceptable nanny-wear in Hyde Park. The setting up of a new Diploma in Childcare by the Lucie Clayton Modelling School, however, might bring about a sudden upsurge of Gianni Versace.

A uniform, of course, works differently when it's worn by a man. The Walton Day Nursery girls were always envied on account of their proximity to the Barracks, and thanks to the impeccable social connections of their employer, Nanny Philipson-Stow, they were asked to all the Balls. Hand-picked young men were sent over for

[65]

sherry at the beginning of the Season. Some of them found inspection by Nanny more harrowing than being reviewed by the Queen.

Few nannies can resist the breath-taking sight of the Household Cavalry exercising in Rotten Row. Resplendent in their scarlet tunics, their cuirasses gleaming, their plumes tossing, and their boots blacked and polished till you can see your face in them, the Guards have been a dominant part of the Knightsbridge scene since the eighteenth century. The Foot Guards had barracks at Hyde Park Corner, but soldiers were also billeted in the village, adding to its boisterous lifestyle. Sometimes they sat on the long benches at the perimeter of the Park having their wigs powdered. This tended to lower the tone, so in 1795, as part of the Prince Regent's scheme to tidy up London, proper cavalry barracks were built near Knightsbridge Green to accommodate six hundred men and five hundred horses.

Today their numbers have been halved. The modern Household Cavalry is an amalgamation of two regiments, the Life Guards, Charles I's personal bodyguard, and the Blues and Royals, formerly the Royal Horse Guards. The Blues wear red plumes, the Life Guards white. Officers' plumes in the Blues are still made of real yak's hair, but because of traffic pollution the white plumes of the Life Guards are now made of washable nylon. The Household Cavalry is an armoured regiment, deployed worldwide on normal reconnaissance tasks. Recently the Life Guards drove tanks in Kuwait. Horses are kept for ceremonial duties, one of which is to 'find' the Queen's Life Guard at Horse Guards, which is the official entrance to Buckingham Palace. Drum horses are bred by Her Majesty the Queen at her own stud and presented to the regiment. The black horses come from Ireland. They are not thoroughbreds, something ordinary members of the public find hard to believe. They are groomed to shining perfection by the troopers. It takes six hours to clean the kit properly: no wonder the nannies approve.

Although few employers can have been as taken aback as the mother who came home to find Nanny asleep stark naked between *two* guardsmen, nannies have lost their hearts to soldiers ever since anyone can remember. Christopher Robin's Nanny, Alice, must have married a Foot Guard since she is always pictured near a Buckingham Palace sentry box. She put it in a nutshell when she said in famously ungrammatical English, 'A soldier's life is terrible hard.'

At Knightsbridge Barracks a trooper's day begins at 6am. He must be in the stables by 6.20. Reveille is at 7am, followed by the regimental watering. All horses which are not to be used that day are exercised before the streets are congested with traffic. Lorry drivers and florists returning from New Covent Garden still stop with old-fashioned courtesy if they meet the Cavalry clattering past the Sloane Street traffic lights. Even in khaki battle-dress they are an awe-inspiring spectacle.

Knightsbridge Barracks is a grand place for horses. The present complex was built in 1966 by Sir Basil Spence. He incorporated the classical pediment from the old building over the entrance gate. Some critics think it contrasts strangely with the livid modern brickwork. There is a forge, ten farriers, a vet and an indoor manège.

[67]

The Blues' stables are on the top floor, the Life Guards' on the ground floor. Tourists on the upper deck of a No. 9 or 52 bus are surprised on hot summer afternoons to find themselves peered at by a row of horses, apparently sunning themselves on a first floor balcony.

Sir Basil's design was limited by the size and shape of the site, so he arrived at the ingenious solution of making troopers' married quarters into a tower block. The flats have fabulous views over the Park – better, insiders say, than those from the Hilton, Lanesborough and Hyde Park Hotels. A guest in the Royal Suite at the Hyde Park Hotel would have to pay £1,762 a night to enjoy the view seen daily by an ordinary soldier's wife, but the tower block is notoriously unpopular with architectural purists, who periodically scream for it to be pulled down. (No one has thought it tactful to consult Prince Charles, but then his Mother is the Colonel-in-Chief.)

This feeling is often shared by cavalry wives. There are thirty-two floors in Sir Basil's tower block and sometimes the lift gets stuck. Wives also grumble that both troopers and officers spend too much time cherishing their mounts and not enough with their families. Eager to placate them, a caring Army has laid on a crèche with NNEB nurses. Hyde Park's beautiful new manège, opened in 1989 by HRH the Princess Royal, is also *strategically* situated beside the swings. Despite the advantages of being bona fide Knightsbridge Women, soldiers' wives require an exceptionally forbearing temperament.

'Do you worship the horse?' asked a young subaltern in the Blues of an actress he was wining and dining in the Cavalry Grill of the Hyde Park Hotel.

Her mind was on a tricky aria from *Lilac Time*. Not realising the question was the preface to a proposal of marriage, she replied, 'Certainly not. My uncle is a Church of England Bishop.'

14

Hatless in the Park

T HE VICTORIAN ERA saw the golden age of riding in the Park. The new young Queen, who as a child had delighted the crowds by unselfconsciously cavorting in a donkey cart in Kensington Palace Gardens, rode often in Rotten Row. She recommended riding as a tonic for the nerves.

The difficulties of mounting in an ankle-length habit can be imagined. They are reflected in the conspicuous number of mounting blocks still spaced about the Park. Two men were needed to get a lady into the saddle, a groom to hold the horse's head, and, if there was no mounting block, a gentleman to hold the lady's foot. Minute instructions for getting on a horse gracefully were issued by Mrs Power O'Donoghue in *Riding for Ladies*. Holding whip and reins in the right hand, a lady was to place her free hand on the gentleman's shoulder, 'he being in the stooping position'. Then, shouting, 'Ready', or 'Go ahead', she was to spring upward, straightening the knee, while he simultaneously rose to an erect position, 'without letting his hand drop in the smallest degree'. The synchronisation required for this operation must have been simply frightful.

If the lady's petticoat brushed his cheek as she flew upwards, the cavalier was, of course, expected to avert his eyes. The robust beauties of the eighteenth century had ridden quite without knickers, but now underclothing complied with the delicacies of the age. 'To expect a habit-cutter to fit a bodice over a seven-and-sixpenny corset with two long bones sticking out,' wrote Mrs Power O'Donoghue severely, was as great an injustice as expecting 'an artist to paint a picture with broken brushes'.

A side-saddle had a crutch round which the rider could delicately hook her right knee. A properly cut habit of good melton cloth covered the knee gracefully. Cheap stuff creased and crumpled. Towards the end of the century a complicated safety skirt was recommended, fastened by only one hook and eye at the waist, so that it gave way if the lady fell off. The idea was to prevent nasty accidents, for if a lady's skirt caught round the pommel of her saddle as she was falling, she could be dragged along head-downwards by the animal's side. Of course, if the safety skirt fell off instead, she revealed her bloomers, and anyone who wore one for hunting was inclined to be cut by the County.

In the 1850s a debate raged through England over whether ladies should hunt at all. 'It leads to flirting, they say – to flirting of a sort which mothers would not approve,' wrote one moralist. Nevertheless prowess in the saddle was a passport to all sorts of self-betterment. Catherine Walters, known as 'Skittles' because she was once employed collecting balls in a skittle-alley, was the daughter of a Liverpool Customs official. She was a brilliant rider and in the late 1850s, when she was eighteen, she moved to London. Her skills were noted by a livery stable-keeper in Bruton Mews, who immediately took her on as one of the 'pretty young horse-breakers'. Just as beauties photographed in G-strings are now used to sell Pirelli tyres, these girls were employed by horse dealers to advertise fine mounts. The stable owners paid for their clothes; their morals were their own concern. They paraded about Tattersall's on sale days and strangely, although a prostitute soliciting in Rotten Row on foot would have been arrested on the spot, those on horseback were considered quite acceptable.

'The Danaes! The Amazons! The lady cavaliers! The horsewomen!' wrote G. A. Sala in *Twice Around the Clock*. 'Can any scene in the world equal Rotten Row in the full tide of the Season? Watch the sylphides as they fly or float past in their ravishing riding habits and intoxicatingly delightful hats; some with the orthodox cylindrical beaver with flowing veil; others with roguish little wide-awakes or cavaliers' hats and green plumes.'

Skittles, who rode in a habit so perfectly cut, and so tightly moulded to her exquisite form that it was rumoured she wore nothing underneath, is generally credited with having introduced the top hat with silk veil into England. In 1862 she began an affair with Lord Hartington, the heir to the Duke of Devonshire. Later that year an article in *The Times* reported that a huge traffic jam in the South Carriage Road had been caused not by the crush of people visiting the International Exhibition, but by a beautiful horsewoman who chose to ride in the rush hour. So sensational was her appearance that it caused the traffic to stop in both directions.

[72]

Catherine Walters was suddenly the most talked-about woman in London society. Wherever she chose to ride or drive became the venue of the moment. She had the status of a modern Supermodel. When her affair with Lord Hartington ended she went to live in Paris, returning to England each autumn to hunt with the Quorn. She continued to practise as a courtesan, which meant respectable ladies could not ask her to their houses, but when the Master of the Quorn's wife forced him to send her home, Skittles commented, 'I don't know why Lady Stamford should object to me. She isn't even the head of our profession. Lady Cardigan is.'

She was soon back in the field and Lord Stamford, admiring her prowess, muttered, 'Damn all jealous women!' She remained the undisputed 'Queen' of Rotten Row until the 1870s, when she was eclipsed by the Empress of Austria, who came over to hunt with the Grafton and rode down the Row on her milk-white Coronation steed.

Towards the end of the century the hard bowler began to replace the top hat for both ladies and men. Between the Wars, however, it was still considered very bad form to ride in the Row in anything but the best cut gear. Sir Walter Gilbey of the gin manufacturing family first marked the decline in standards in the 1930s, when young men with sleek hair began cantering about in jodhpurs so baggy they reminded him of an old-fashioned cycling suit. They also rode *without hats*, and some of the ladies followed their deplorable example.

'Suppose the King appeared, or any member of the Royal Family. What an insult that would be,' objected

Sir Walter. He became an acknowledged expert on riding dress and would lean upon the Park railings shouting insults at people who were incorrectly turned out. The papers adored him, frequently publishing headlines about his outbursts:

Baronet and Hatless Riders – Rank Bad Taste
Volley of Criticism from the Footpath

On one occasion he was accused of being a snob. He thundered that he was no such thing.

'Let everybody come. I want only to see a fine tradition preserved. This place is famed all over the world. It makes me furious, when people wantonly seek to destroy it.'

Sir Walter's tirades became so celebrated that a nephew of his, Ronald Gilbey, wrote a ballad called *Riding in the Row.*

Each mother to her daughter, as she dresses her with care
Says, 'Try and keep yourself done up, you'd better now beware.
Sir Walter will be in the Park, now just you think of that
You'll know him by his buttonhole and curly bowler hat.'

The elegant railings upon which Sir Walter leaned to deliver his broadsides were removed in 1941 and melted down for munitions. Scrap metal was highly valued during the War. Even Queen Mary, down at Badminton, did her bit, energetically leading foraging parties to poke out old iron bedsteads which had been thrown into ditches. As

[74]

part of the Rotten Row Tercentenary celebrations in 1990, Neil Mitchell launched an appeal to restore the bollards which had lined the Row since the eighteenth century. A mile of replica railings comprising 950 bollards was set up, lit by twenty gas lamps in the Victorian style. Firms and individuals paid £200 for a bollard inscribed with the donor's name, and £3000 for a gas lamp. Subscribers ranged from the Duke of Wellington to Barbara Cartland.

Her Majesty the Queen was patron of the Tercentenary. Hyde Park saw the greatest cavalcade since the Coronation. Ladies of the Side-Saddle Association took part in the parade, along with brewers' drays, the Household Cavalry, the King's Troop, the Royal Horse Artillery and the Metropolitan Police. Splendid letters erupted in *The Times*, hoping that riding dress might once again conform to pre-War standards. The Civil Service Riding Club grandly pointed out that *its* rules required members to wear hacking jackets and breeches or jodhpurs, a collar and tie, and a British Standards approved riding hat. Riders had been seen slopping about, said *The Times*, in very odd clothing, including jeans and tennis shoes.

This posed a problem for the two remaining commercial stable owners near the Park: Richard Briggs and Ross Nye, who both have riding schools in Bathurst Mews. They could scarcely turn customers away, when some were innocent tourists who had flown from the antipodes to ride the famous four-and-a-half mile circuit of newly-sanded bridleways and failed to pack a hacking jacket. Richard devised a uniquely British compromise. He printed a brochure showing his beautiful wife, Basia, riding casually through the Park *in a cardigan*. Inside, however, a carefully worded sentence warned that Standard riding clothes must be worn in the manège.

Before the War there were many livery stables south of the Park. The last to close was Lilo Blum's in Grosvenor Crescent Mews. A much-loved horsewoman, she had taught riding in the Park for forty-five years. She believed in the old-fashioned discipline of a coin between the knee and the saddle, so that pupils learned to stick on. Zsa Zsa Gabor, the Kennedy children and Pavarotti all rode with her when they came to London. She once galloped down Sloane Street to chase and arrest a handbag thief. Sadly, just before her lease expired in 1988, a careless workman knocked over a blow-lamp and her stables burned down.

A great to-do erupted. The freehold of Lilo's stables belonged to the Duke of Westminster, a countryman at heart, but in this instance an urban landlord to other tenants in Grosvenor Crescent Mews who objected to the incessant clatter of hooves. Mighty rivalries ensued and great powers were invoked. There had been horses in the Mews since 1766, when the Duke of Buccleuch kept a coaching stable there. English Heritage promptly listed the building, which had a Victorian tack room, stalls and hayboxes, all of which survived the fire. The London Tourist Board then joined the fray, saying, 'It would be a great pity to see London's central riding school disbanded.' Lilo, who had helped establish Riding for the Disabled in the Royal Mews at Buckingham Palace, wrote to the Queen. Sympathetically the Queen explained she could not intervene between the Duke and his leaseholder. Westminster Council then took the bit between its teeth and dilly-dallied over granting the Duke 'change of use'. He wanted to make it into an art gallery, but English Heritage put their foot down over any attempt to tamper with the hayboxes.

By the time planning permission was finally granted in 1994, the Queen had created a wonderful diversion by falling off her horse while riding in Windsor Great Park in a headscarf. The headscarf did not conform to British Safety Standards and a completely non-equestrian press was up in arms. Ironically, as Colonel-in-Chief of the Household Cavalry the Queen had for years reviewed troops in a natty little black hat without exciting a murmur.*

---

*The hat was designed by the Danish milliner Aage Thaarup in the style of a regimental tricorne. In Australia the twist with which the Queen secures her headscarf is called 'the Knightsbridge Knot'.

15

Pond Life

WE TAKE POND LIFE seriously in England. It is included in the National Curriculum of our schools. In popularity it outstrips Music and Art in the better sort of State primary schools, where seven-year-olds lobby for the post of Frog Monitor. Old Kensington people swear they remember the days when there *were* frogs in the Round Pond, and speak mistily of afternoons spent, with Nanny's approval, ladling gelatinous lumps of frogspawn into jam jars.

Changed eco-systems have done for all that. The sperm count of London frogs has gone down and poisonous algae are a common hazard facing whichever government department controls the Royal Parks for a given span. Experts claim the trouble is caused by Global Warming. This myth survives even when rival experts have appeared on television the previous evening to say it has been the wettest, coldest August on record.

Poisonous algae make bathing unsafe in most parts of the Serpentine, but around the Lido, the section of the lake opposite Prince of Wales Gate, the water is chlorinated from June to September. Nude bathing is absolutely forbidden, though lady members of the Serpentine

Swimming Club have been allowed to swim topless since 1987. One of the Lido's treasures is a sepia photograph of London's first WPC chasing seven naked urchins out of the water in the hot summer of 1926. They had climbed over the railings and disrobed without paying.

The intrepid Early Morning Swimming Club meets between 6.30am and 9.30am – *all year round*. Its members include several bona fide Channel Swimmers. Most of them have such toned up immune systems that the poisonous algae retreat when they see them coming. The Club has been going for 132 years; one or two of the current regulars are octogenarians. They race for silver cups on Saturday mornings.

Indigenous Brits make up a large part of the Club's membership. They pay £7 a year for the risky privilege of swimming in unchlorinated waters from October to May, and are intensely proud of their freedom to do so. All members sign a disclaimer to say they will not prosecute the Department of National Heritage if they contract unhygienic diseases. Resident Americans find this one of the many perplexing aspects of the English Way of Life. They prefer to pay inordinate sums to swim in the super-chlorinated waters at the health clubs of adjacent hotels. Their children have adopted the pitch south of the Lido for playing softball. For the benefit of Lido members and non-Europeans, a cooked English breakfast is served at the Waterside Café all day. Slimmers and the cholesterol-conscious are advised to abstain.

Londoners call the softball pitch Little America and the North Shore of the Serpentine Jeddah High Street. The demarcations are voluntary. No one understands why

[79]

London's first WPC chasing naked urchins out of the
water in the hot summer of 1926.

Middle Eastern visitors always promenade on the North Shore and Americans migrate to the South. Sometimes the Arab visitors shoot home videos of the Canada Geese. The ladies are some of the most smartly dressed women in London, as they shop in the fashion capitals of the world, but their menfolk prefer to stick to traditional clothing. Even in wet weather, they retain their sun-proof headcloths with the elegant black rope trim.

The Canada Geese pose a constant problem for the authorities. They crop grass, increase and multiply at a terrific rate, pile up excrement at the Nannies' end of the Round Pond and generally make a nuisance of themselves. Mr Kerr, the former Keeper of the Royal Park Birds, holds the private opinion that they should be classified as vermin, but the Department of National Heritage wilfully persists in classifying them as game birds. Mr Worthylake, who is one of the Hyde Park Supervisors, sends two motorised road-sweepers to clean up after them every day. Spasmodically the *Evening Standard* runs features to suggest the geese should be fed contraceptive pills.

The South Shore of the Serpentine, Fisherman's Keep, is the territory of the native English. Persevering anglers catch bream, perch, tench and roach, with which the Department of the Environment proudly re-stocked the Lake before they were ousted by the trendier Department of National Heritage. Permit-holders pay for the privilege of catching the fish, but they are honour-bound to throw them back again. The system is based on the British ethic of Fair Play, which often puzzles habitués of the more cosmopolitan North Shore.

Very occasionally the two cultures clash. Mrs Green,

the owner of a North Carolina Wood Duck, used to take her pet to the Round Pond on Sundays. She was a constant source of delight to afternoon strollers and in particular to the Kensington Kite-Fliers, who assemble near the Pond on the Knightsbridge side of the Broad Walk. The duck travelled in a weaver basket and would waddle back to its mistress after a nice swim with the mallard and teal. One Sunday a small dark-haired child started throwing stones at the duck. Possibly he was impelled by the genes of his ancestors, who had speared birds on the banks of the Nile, but Mrs Green, believing him to be English, commanded him to stop. He seemed intent on killing the duck and redoubled his efforts.

Following the fine old British tradition of 'spare the rod and spoil the child', Mrs Green picked up the disobedient boy and threw him headlong into the Pond. Mayhem ensued. It was not clear whether those in charge of the child were his parents or his brothers and sisters. They did not speak English and they certainly did not seem to appreciate that in the United Kingdom bird life is *venerated*. The police refused to press charges and Mrs Green stalked triumphantly off, carrying her duck in its basket. The crowd applauded tremendously.

Responsibility for what goes on in the Park and the Gardens is shared by the environmental departments of the Royal Borough which supervises Kensington Gardens east of the Broad Walk, and the City of Westminster which is responsible for the rest. They try to outdo each other with ingenious solutions to matters of vital import like litter, dog waste and the colour traditional gas lamps should be painted. Kensington holds open days, when the public are invited to inspect its bottle-banks. When Lord Strathclyde was the Parliamentary Under-Secretary of State for the Environment he was a popular figure at press launches being such a good public speaker. The lamenting was universal when they moved him to Trade and Industry. Westminster once photographed Lady Porter, then Chairperson of their Council, driving a motorised street-sweeper, but she didn't have the glamour of an hereditary peer.

On the Westminster side *two* councillors are required to serve the needs of the vast catchment area. Their territory includes the Round Pond, the Serpentine and Long Water, which means they have control of the Peter Pan statue – an ethnic outrage, since there is printed evidence that he was reared in the Royal Borough. The Councils overlap with the Department of National Heritage, which is in charge of ducks, and the Royal Parks Police, who have powers over noise, public decency and unauthorised roller-skating. Persons who drown in the Serpentine come under the jurisdiction of the Knightsbridge coroner, who has removed to SE1.

In the 1920s a medical student taking an early morning dip came across a dead Chinaman in the Serpentine. The spirit of scientific enquiry so got the better of him that, forgetting the procedure for the recovery of cadavers, he set the body astride his bike and wheeled it home across the Park, eager to perform an autopsy.

'Normally', said a present-day spokesman for the Royal Parks Constabulary, 'anyone finding a body in the Serpentine has a duty to wonder how it got there. They should call us and we'd inform the CID.'

[83]

Apart from the Queen, the only person entitled to drive a carriage across Hyde Park without first obtaining special permission is the Duke of St Albans, the hereditary Grand Falconer of England. So far nobody has persuaded him to try.

16

The World of Work

A S WELL AS worrying that the Canada Geese should
be fed contraceptive pills, the *Evening Standard*
every now and then has a good old worry about
lurking mafiosi. Its recent preoccupation is with the Rus-
sian Mafia, who are suspected of trying to get a hold on
the housing market. It is very unlikely. London has
enough mafiosi of its own. Take our porter, George, the
undisputed leader of the secret network which recom-
mends door-keepers, security guards and Spanish char-
ladies to every prestige block south of the Serpentine and
west of Hyde Park Corner.

George has a wonderful way with the give-away magazines. When the rubbish chute gets blocked, he takes a
pile of them to the top floor and drops them down the
aperture. This serves a dual purpose. Few bags of garbage
are so immoveable that they cannot be dislodged by
twenty-four copies of *Boardroom*, and by disposing of these
as they arrive George does not have to add to the mass
of free paper thrust daily through our letter boxes.

It has to be admitted that the give-away magazines are
getting better. Originally it was a foregone conclusion
that nobody in their right minds would want to read

them. Most were owned by little gangs (dare we say mafiosi?) of house agents, intent on gingering up the market for real estate. That is, they contained more advertising matter than features, but recently, through listing more and more information about local events, they have become acceptable substitutes for parish magazines. Stung by the contempt and loathing heaped upon them by bona fide NUJ members, who have the monopoly of jobs on *Tatler* and *Harpers & Queen*, they have begun to publish ravishing cover pictures.

Christopher Cooke, the publisher of *The Hill* and *SW Magazine*, once accidentally used a picture by a *Vogue* photographer. Set upon by the mighty organisation of Condé Nast, he was ordered by a judge to pay damages, but having insufficient assets he made restitution in kind by publishing free subscription advertisements for *Tatler*.

After George has done the rubbish chutes, he takes Heather's dog Yeti to the Park. Yeti is a Polish sheep dog, so called because when he hasn't rolled about in the mud he is pure white and reminds anyone whose memory goes that far back of the Abominable Snowman said to rove the Himalayas making footprints. Heather is Heather Hammond, late of Carlton Office Services. In the employment world she was the inventor of off-beat networking and, as such, a legend in her time. The Carlton agency was pre-Sloane and served the House of Lords through the sixties, the seventies and into the eighties. Its best-loved premises were in Harriet Walk at the time when the florists Pulbrook & Gould were at the Harvey Nicks end of Sloane Street. Lady Pulbrook's back door was adjacent to Heather's office front. In the seventies, when fur coats were acceptable presents from grateful oil sheikhs, it was common after 5.30pm to see one of Heather's girls, mink-coated to the ankles, *rummaging* like a bag-lady through Lady P's bins for a few old orchids.

In winter Heather ran a soup kitchen for broke debs who had blown their lunch money on Hermès scarves.

'She always found lovely people for you to work for,' said Jilly Ashcroft, remembering the glamorous old days. 'One man used to send his chauffeur in the Rolls to pick me up. It was fine until Heather went to Scotland for a week, leaving me to mind her cat, Jinx. One morning, just as we'd stopped at the Sloane Street traffic light, Jinxie went berserk. She clung to the chauffeur, peed on the front seat, clawed the back, which was upholstered in cream leather, and mewed piteously. The chauffeur threw Brut aftershave on the carpet and it went from maroon to soft pink.'

Little accidents of this sort never seemed to mar the agency's reputation, and Jinx became a regular feature of Knightsbridge life. She couldn't bear to spend the day cooped up in a flat, so was taken to the office every morning. In winter she travelled in a cat basket on the No. 9 bus. In summer Heather cycled to work. Jinx would start off in the bicycle basket, but round about the Albert Hall she would leap onto her mistress's shoulder and soon became one of the sights of Rotten Row. The *Evening Standard* photographed the pair, Heather pedalling furiously with Jinx above her coat collar, arching her back against the skyline.

'Carlton girls were always well-dressed,' recalls Suzy Butterfield. 'We had the reputation of being Ritzy. We made little economies in some ways, but never on clothes. The girls loved Heather. She remembered all our preferences. She would never have *dreamed* of asking me to work in Ascot Week. Jilly went to another agency once for temp work and they sent her to Oxford Street. I mean, *Oxford Street*, can you imagine? Nothing like that ever happened at Carlton. You'd be sent to the House of Lords, and everybody would ask you down for the weekend. You had to have good clothes.

'The employers adored Heather, too. She was so *social*. She'd pick up the phone and say, "I've just lost Jinx, my cat, on the Knightsbridge Underground. She's been spotted travelling 'Up' on the 'Down' escalator. You want two girls for Friday? Ninety words a minute, yes, of course." She always delivered the goods and Heather's girls could *spell*.'

In those heady days before the fax machine and the word processor revolutionised the business world, nobody wanted a permanent job. P.A. Management was quartered in Bowater House and the Independent Broadcasting Authority was opposite Harrods. Both employed armies of bright typists and pretty secretaries. Management was viewed as rather lacklustre. Men in management didn't play polo and some of them had rather flash cars.

'P.A. men,' said Jilly, 'were the dullest bosses. I remember a man who didn't even know my name. He would call me in and say, "Miss Um . . . Take a letter, please." Then he'd sit looking out over the Park, dictating with his back to me. After a fortnight I couldn't stand it, so one day I went in when he buzzed, waited till he turned his back and said, "I'm sitting behind you. I've just taken

[88]

all my clothes off. I'm totally naked and you don't even know my name." He swivelled round, his mouth open with shock, and said, "Miss Ummmmm—!" The next day I got an enormous bunch of flowers and he'd even rung Heather to get my name right on the card.'

Grosvenor Guides' girls were also crème de la crème. The company was started by Judy Hoad, who trained at the Royal Academy of Music to be a pianist. She wanted to be a concert performer, but at the end of the War found she was more in demand for shows like *The Student Prince* and the *Beggar's Opera*.

'Fay Compton was my godmother, so I suppose it was natural. I came out in 1919 and was presented at Court to Queen Mary just after the Great War. Nobody thought they would have to work then. We used to learn the waltz and the foxtrot and go to the tea dances at the Knightsbridge Hotel. My husband drove a tube train in the General Strike. We used to go to dinner with the Burbage girls, when Sir Richard, the Managing Director of Harrods, had a flat on the roof.'

She founded Grosvenor Guides in the sixties, and moved to Harriet Walk in the seventies.

'All my girls were ladies. They drove four-door saloons and had to pass the exams set by the British Tourist Authority. I remember one couple who wanted to be taken from the Hilton to do Oxford and Cambridge in one day. I thought, "Gosh, how ghastly," but they explained they wanted to start a chain of restaurants. They were quite charming but I'm afraid they were the *hamburger* people.'

Judy was in her seventies when the little company was

in its heyday, but the lure of show business was too strong. She went back to piano playing and at ninety was doing the lunchtime jazz spot at the Pizza on the Park. Made redundant at ninety-one, she quit Knightsbridge to play jazz at Kettners Restaurant in Soho.

17

Doing the Flowers

ON THE NORTH SIDE of Knightsbridge stood a
fashionable chapel, famous for runaway weddings.
It was on the site of the present-day café Ange-
lique, roughly opposite the Minema. For some reason it
was the only church in London exempt from calling the
banns, so it became a sort of Gretna Green of the Home
Counties.

As the chapel was on the coaching route, kidnapped
heiresses in torn lace and mud-spattered satin regularly
tumbled out of post-chaises onto its doorstep and were
led straight up to the altar. They were often pursued by
avenging fathers, but could be conveniently spirited away
to one of the many disreputable inns in the district,
patronised by highwaymen and the local soldiery.

Although technically Holy Trinity, the church was
always called 'Knightsbridge Chapel'. A leper hospital in
Elizabethan times, it withstood the Civil War, and usefully
specialised in mass funerals during the Plague. Though it
stuck to one creed it tended to change shape, being a
prey to ambitious architects. The early Victorians pulled
down its classical pediment and minaretted bell-tower,
fitting it with 650 pews and a shining new clerestory in

the high Gothic style, but its heyday was in the eighteenth century. With a gin shop on either side, Knightsbridge Chapel was known for decades as the Heaven between two Hells.

Some of the heiresses who married there were pregnant, others merely rich. Many local inns had secret passages, leading to escape routes through the stables. In 1846 when the Half-Way House, a ramshackle hostelry used by travellers quenching their thirst on the long journey from Kensington to London, was demolished to make room for Prince of Wales Gate, a staircase was found concealed in the thickness of the wall. Hasty unions could be consummated at such premises. When father turned up, the bride had already 'disappeared' and, since husbands had inalienable rights over their wives' property, so, probably, had half his estate.

On account of the pregnancies, many of the marriages recorded in the register had 'secret' written in the margin, but as Knightsbridge was in the Parish of St Margaret's Westminster, which caters for Members of Parliament, a few Society Weddings took place there too. Sir Robert Walpole married one of the Lord Mayor of London's daughters at Knightsbridge Chapel. She brought him a handsome dowry but promptly spent it all on jewels. She also made him the father of that redoubtable old gossip, Horace Walpole. Pepys' friend Sir Samuel Morland was even more unfortunate. He married a Mrs Mary Ayliss, whom he took for an heiress, only to find she was a coachman's daughter, 'not worth a shilling'.

With its picaresque associations the chapel would have been a popular venue for Society Weddings today, but in an enthusiastic burst of boundary moving it was pulled down at the turn of the century and removed to Prince Consort Road, to serve the spiritual needs of Kensington Gore. No longer 'Knightsbridge Chapel', it became the *third* Holy Trinity in the area, and is a source of terrible confusion to lost tourists trying to find the stop for the C1 Hoppa bus.

You would think that with three Holy Trinities in a half-mile radius of each other, the Anglican Church was hedging its bets. God in Nine Persons, so to speak, watching over one of London's costliest tracts of real estate. It doesn't muddle *only* the tourists. Whole taxis full of wedding guests have been known to go astray. A contingent in morning dress, destined for a formal do at Holy Trinity Sloane Street, once sat through an entire saxophone recital at the evangelical Holy Trinity Brompton, before realising they were at the wrong wedding. They kept wondering why the bridesmaids wore denim.

H.T.B., which sometimes attracts one thousand worshippers to Sunday Evensong, is heavily into marriage. It has parking facilities and is mentioned as a suitable venue in *The Sloane Ranger Handbook*. Wedding photographers adore it for its glorious garden, full of birds and bluebells, looked after by four green-fingered ladies who also act as guides at the Chelsea Physic Garden. They have won several prizes, but garden in radically different styles. The walled bed running up the drive, which is a mass of snowdrops in early spring, presents problems in summer, when the hosepipe won't stretch to the far end. Lady

Glenkinglas, who tends it, aims for a wilderness effect; a passing tramp once offered to clear her 'weeds'.

Holy Trinity Sloane Street has a Burne-Jones window, lovingly set up by William Morris. It is handy for Peter Jones and the General Trading Co, two fashionable places to keep bridal lists, but it doesn't make the *Handbook* on account of being surrounded by a prodigious number of yellow lines. The choral scholars from Hill House sing there every third Sunday and it sells the widest range of Charity Christmas Cards in all London. It does bona fide Society Weddings regardless of the parking.

You can always tell a Society Wedding by the cow parsley. Whole buckets of the stuff clutter the vestry floor, sucking up water so it won't droop when it's stuck in Oasis. Cow parsley in Knightsbridge lends a nice country touch, so much less urban than gypsophila, and in the eyes of top florists more 'U'. It reassures the bridal pair, conjuring memories of golden afternoons spent in ineffably English buttercup meadows. You couldn't get a buttercup into Oasis. It would wilt.

Once upon a time two big arrangements of lilies on the altar, and rosebuds on the pew ends were all that was needed, even for the grandest wedding, but nowadays foliage is compulsory. Top florists get asked to do whole *archways* of lilies, threaded with myrtle and jasmine, to say nothing of *thickets* of standard roses, and avenues of potted marguerites, to line the red carpet down which the bride will progress. Whole teams of decorators work overnight, and pew ends get shaggier every season, competing for a mention in *Jennifer's Diary* by Lady Celestria Noel.

[94]

At such a wedding my son's godfather's uncle (an Ampleforth monk, so perforce a Social Catholic) once turned to bless the happy couple and saw to his horror that the bride could not get back. She had walked down the aisle on the arm of her *thin* father, precariously skirting the pew ends. Now encumbered with a *wide-ish* husband, she stood marooned in a sea of blossom. The organist played the Wedding March twice before the poor woman made a dash for it, scattering petals and slicing off lumps of Oasis with layers of stiffened tulle petticoat.

Despite the omnipresent Trinities, the parish church of Knightsbridge is St Paul's, Wilton Place. Teetering on the borders of Belgravia, it is noted for smart weddings and was the first church in London to permit full scale rehearsals. This dated from the time of the Bright Young Things, when weddings became progressively theatrical and Noël Coward and Tallulah Bankhead were on all the guest lists. It was the Age of Jazz, and daring couples sometimes substituted Louis Armstrong for Mendelssohn. Almost the last people to marry secretly in Knightsbridge were the parents of the present Lord Bath. Their parents thought they were too young, so the sixth Marquis, then Lord Weymouth, used his middle name, Frederick, instead of Henry, and his wife Daphne used her second name, Winifred, for the banns. Later, with the bride in a Norman Hartnell dress of white net over silver lamé, they were remarried ceremoniously in St Martin-in-the-Fields, but St Paul's became so popular for Society Weddings that when the Berkeley Hotel moved to its 'new' premises, the architect designed the banqueting entrance to face the vestry door.

[95]

Now encumbered with a wideish husband, she stood marooned in a sea of blossom.

Weddings in Knightsbridge have become such big business that top florists form a 'holy trinity' all of their own. Felton, which had the royal appointment to Edward VII and Queen Alexandra in 1902, have been in their shop with the black and white awnings opposite the Brompton Oratory for over sixty years. They invented the Brompton Non-Drip Window Box and were pioneers of indoor plant care.

'My Dear Lady Portarlington, you have let all that lovely cyclamen droop. I shan't sell you another unless you promise to take care of it,' the great Mr Rutledge, one of the firm's most adored directors, would chide.

Moyses Stevens, who do the Grosvenor House Hotel and have a concession in Harrods, have held the Queen Mother's warrant since 1940. It is proudly displayed above their premises near Holy Trinity, Sloane Street. Her Majesty still sends personal notes to thank them for arrangements she finds especially charming.

The doyenne of London's flower ladies, however, is Lady Pulbrook. When her husband died in 1954 she opened a shop with Rosamund Gould at the Harvey Nichols end of Sloane Street. It quickly became known for unusual flowers. When other florists sold gladioli, Pulbrook & Gould offered parrot tulips and little bunches of widow iris. When the rents tripled Lady Pulbrook moved to an elegant arcade beside the General Trading Co. A veteran of three royal weddings, she is the High Apostle of foliage, and runs a floristry school dead opposite Moyses Stevens, with whom she competes in a spirit of friendly rivalry. A vivacious eighty-year-old, she still goes to the Nine Elms Flower Market at 4am on days when she thinks

[97]

her buyer needs a rest. Foliage is specially grown for her in English country gardens, and she has a deceptively artless way with the cow parsley.

She keeps up a constant flow of funny stories about the flower trade. Her most hair-raising experience was when Sir Laurence Olivier's funeral coincided with a long-planned arrangement to meet the Queen, who was to open Dorton House, a College of Further Education for blind teenagers in Sevenoaks.

'The Queen was in the morning in Kent. Larry's funeral was in the afternoon in Sussex. Joan Plowright had asked me to do a miniature garden on top of the coffin and to place in it a little Bible which Larry had loved.'

The Bible was handed over to Lady Pulbrook the night before. Dressed in pink for the Queen, she had a black outfit for the funeral discreetly stowed in the back of her car. The Queen, who is never late, was late, and as Chairman of the Royal London Society for the Blind, Lady Pulbrook could scarcely leave before her Sovereign. Worse still, the Queen *enjoyed* Dorton House and lingered, chatting.

Eventually Her Majesty left. Lady Pulbrook was driven at breakneck speed through the highways and byways of England. She arrived in the nick of time, but without changing into the black suit. Still in vibrant pink, she rushed forward with the little Bible, and was confronted by 'a whole hedgerow of photographers. More than I'd ever seen in my life. More than for the Queen.'

As the whole event was televised, she was teased for months to come.

18

Children and Dogs

CHILDREN AND DOGS frequently get bracketed in the Englishwoman's mind. Both respond to short, sharp commands. Both need to be fed and house-trained. Both require continuous exercise, even in wet weather.

Foreigners mysteriously think this means the English don't love their children. Dog-lovers know them to be wrong. We love our children and *dote* on our dogs. A very small Chinese child in Kensington Gardens once gravely put me right on the idea that we are the only nation on earth which loves dogs. She told me the Chinese love dogs too. 'People think the Chinese eat their dogs,' but, she said, this was only in times of famine, and so great was the Chinese love of dogs that even in the worst famine China had ever known, starving people would not eat their own dogs. They ate their neighbours' dogs.

Children in Knightsbridge are surprisingly nice. They are an international set nowadays, which means some of them have foreign parents and experience us as an *alien culture*, but they still take exercise in Hyde Park, sail radio-controlled boats on the Round Pond and play in the Children's Playground near the outdoor manège out-side the Cavalry Barracks. In the weeks before the Royal Tournament they get to watch the Royal Horse Artillery practising the Musical Ride for free. The horses and riders perform figures of eight, while dragging a gun-carriage of the type used at the Battle of Waterloo. Even American kids are impressed. Most local children have perpetual access to Harrods' Toy Department, which stocks the most expensive toys in the world, but also does a steady line in plastic dinosaurs for pocket-money customers. They let you have free goes on the Nintendo computer games too, and all this makes the children of Knights-bridge Woman believe they will inherit the Earth.

Dogs get a good deal, too. When our porter, George, takes Yeti to the Round Pond at half-past seven, before the Spanish charlady mafia arrives, he meets a very nice class of dog-walker. The dog-walkers come in waves, and the early surge includes two MPs, four Peers of the Realm, a titled lady kite-flyer and Somebody Who Comes From The Palace with a charcoal-coloured shih-tzu. You get such well-mannered dogs, too. The rabbits never run away from the First Wave. They sit and peer through the railings, aristocratically sure of themselves. They know a caring dog-owner when they see one, and that the dogs are too well fed to go for raw bunny. Anyway, nowadays it wouldn't be politically correct, and having attended an Animal Rights Meeting at which the best fed animals were the police horses, I confidently predict that Vegan Dog Food will soon hit the market.

The Second Wave in Kensington Palace Gardens are the Professionals. Trained celebrity-spotters have sometimes caught a glimpse of Nigel Dempster, the *Daily Mail* gossip columnist, being pulled along by five Pekingese. The third lot are the genuine Dog-Walkers, who do it for a living and are now one of the most highly-paid workforces in the capital. They arrive between 9am and 11am with whole teams of dogs, enough dogs, George says, to pull a husky sledge to Alaska. Sometimes he feels the temptation to shout, 'Mush!'

Top dog-walkers all have portable telephones so that the owners can call several times a day to enquire if their charges are all right. One Chihuahua was dropped off every morning with her own bottles of Evian water, and the owner phoned anxiously to check she hadn't been lapping at muddy puddles. Stools are a great worry; owners sometimes ring up at lunchtime to ask if they are all right, but it is of course an offence for a dog to foul a footpath and the Royal Parks provide discreet dark green bins with 'Dog Waste' written on them in lovely gold lettering to ease the situation. In spite of this Japanese tourists sometimes mistake them for postboxes.

The Royal Borough launched its part in the cleaner parks scheme with the usual flamboyance. Lord Strathclyde came down from Scotland *again* and made a speech to say that the Department of the Environment aimed 'to make scooping the poop second nature to Britain's dog owners'. A leaflet called 'Scoop the Poop' was launched on the same day and distributed nationwide, though you don't see many of those hard, shiny plastic scoops in Kensington Gardens. We're very environment-conscious here in the Royal Borough and go much more for the biodegradable bag which can be slipped discreetly out of a mac pocket.

A couple of years ago there was an attempt to curtail dogs' access to Kensington Gardens. The whole Town was in an immediate uproar. Even the American colony, south of the Serpentine, joined in. The Department of National Heritage appointed a review group to improve the Royal Parks. It was suggested dogs should have access but be kept on leads. The Royal Parks' Dog Owners Association was set up forthwith. It started with twenty members in a Chelsea drawing-room, but word got round and the membership soared to 961 almost overnight. Sub-committees assembled near the Waterside Café by the Lido, where there is a portrait of the Queen in a yellow dress, with two strings of pearls and a corgi on a Buckingham Palace sofa.

The review group, which had been heckled everywhere it went by Brian Sewell, the *Evening Standard*'s art critic, caved in and Nigel Dempster bared his fangs with a piece against unauthorised cyclists in Kensington Gardens, who harmed dogs and menaced pedestrians. It shows you what Knightsbridge Woman in battle array can stir up.

One dog famous in English fiction was Nana, who looked after the Darling family who flew off to Never-Never Land with a boy called Peter Pan. Very old Knightsbridge Women will tell you Peter Pan lived in Kensington Gardens. He was a Betwixt-and-Between. That is, born a baby, he was brought up by birds on the island in the middle of the Serpentine. He couldn't fly because he had lost faith, and his mentor was an old crow called Solomon Caw. Peter Pan didn't wear a nightgown, and had dubious relations with a little girl called Maisie, who dressed in *fur* (not even fake fur) and some day all these facts will be unearthed as part of a learned PhD thesis on Gender Studies.

Very young Knightsbridge Women know only that Peter Pan was a character in a movie by Walt Disney. It had a politically incorrect bias, because it featured too many lost boys. A drunken actress at a party might tell you it would have been better if Hook had been played by a woman; Equity *should* have complained; and that for half the price of a dress by Issey Miyake, she would have rewritten the script in a way less offensive to the Equal Opportunities Commission.

Things were simpler in 1904 when J. M. Barrie wrote *Peter Pan* as a stage play, and children believed in fairies. He followed it up with a book. Then came another book, *Peter Pan in Kensington Gardens*. Later, when he was *Sir* James Barrie, the royalties of the two books went to the upkeep of the Great Ormond Street Children's Hospital. His friend Sir George Frampton also made a statue of Peter Pan, which appeared suddenly one May morning in Kensington Gardens. Both men were famous, so the Ministry of Works wanted an unveiling, but Barrie and Frampton saw into the hearts of children, who in those days looked for fairies in the flowers beds, so there was no unveiling. Peter Pan just appeared spontaneously blowing his pipes in cold cast bronze at the bit in the Gardens where you can find cowslips and sometimes a white bluebell.

There are squirrels and rabbits and mice around the statue. One of the fairies is sticking her bottom out very

[103]

rudely, and tucked away at the back, where only the curious can see, is an animal which is neither a squirrel nor a rabbit but a bit of both. To this day, although a notice by Long Water tells you about Cormorants and Pied Wagtails, the Shoveler Duck, and the ballet-like mating routine of the Great Crested Grebe, there is no plaque which boasts that the statue was made by Sir George Frampton, and tourists have to look in their guide books to find the name of the actress who posed for Peter Pan.*

Although children no longer believe in fairies, marketing entrepreneurs believe deeply in children, who in Knightsbridge are a serious consumer group. The most noticeable children in the area all seem to go to Hill House, which has been London's most famous prep school ever since Prince Charles went there. It is still terribly English with Latin on the curriculum, and the fourteen choral scholars, who sing like angels at Holy Trinity Sloane Street, bring a lump to the throat at Christmas time.

Hill House has no playing fields of its own, and the children are brought up not to grumble. They go streaming off to the Park, to outlying sports grounds for cricket and rugger, and all over London for swimming, fencing, judo and ballet lessons. Shoppers see crocodiles of children in the distinctive Hill House uniform of gold jerseys and brown knickerbockers three or four times a day as they cross and re-cross Hans Place. Some shoppers

---

*Nina Boucicault, who was thirty-seven years old when she played Peter Pan in the first production of the play in December 1904.

spot them so often that there is a theory that one class does no work at all, but parades round London like film extras to advertise the school. Most of the children look so happy that tourists, foxed by the whimsical uniform, think they *are* film extras and start peering round for the cameras.

The BBC once made a documentary about Hill House, called 'Knickerbockers in Knightsbridge', so it is widely known that the school is in London and Switzerland; that the Headmaster, Colonel Townend, commutes between the two, and that all pupils learn winter sports. Swimming and rock climbing are compulsory. Half the children are English and half are foreign, because the Colonel believes children should be educated for an international world. This means half the parents are foreign too. Ex-patriate employees of mighty companies, many live in rented property and are still in deep culture shock over the uniquely British combination of high rents and primitive bathrooms. The Department of Trade and Industry has even put out a special leaflet to placate outraged Americans over the nationwide absence of power showers. It is even worse for people from Abu Dhabi, who think gold plate is the natural coating for bath taps.

Although Hill House is generally considered smart, not all the parents have loads-a-money, and the ones who *have* are not encouraged to show it off. This further puzzles parents from countries where it is still a fine and proper thing to be rich. They do not understand the mystique of underplayed wealth, and wonder why the Hill House fees, which include lunch, tea and travel to Switzerland, should be so proudly alleged to be among the lowest in London for a private preparatory school. The prospectus really *boasts* about this.

Another of the crocodiles crisscrossing the Park is the St Nicholas Montessori School, who wear lovely scarlet tracksuits and white T-shirts, which match the Life Guards when the children play near Rotten Row. The founders of their school, two very English ladies called Miss Humphrey and Miss Child, were among Maria Montessori's first disciples. They made such a success of the centre at Prince's Gate that when Maria Montessori died her son Mario asked them for funds. England had just gone through a War and, thinking the place was quite threadbare enough, Miss Humphrey and Miss Child with restrained dignity refused to pay up. They were expelled from the Movement, but now that the Montessori method has become fashionable schools are sprouting up everywhere. A rich dog-walker who knows all London's secrets tells me that, since the Lloyds crash, merchant bankers' wives are turning to Montessori teaching and we may even expect a Montessori School in Thurloe Square.

Give the child the Right Thing at the Right Time, and its interest will be kindled forever. This great Montessori precept has been rapturously embraced by the marketing directors of sw1. Harrods' Toys now stretches voluptuously through *four* departments while Harvey Nichols stocks two hundred different shoe designs for discerning little girls. Knightsbridge is a wonderful place to awaken a child's natural lust for learning.

At the dearer end of Sloane Street a wealth of shops aims to help little girls develop a healthy sense of

Contemporary Values. Oilily, a branch of the successful Dutch chain, claim their range is for colour-hungry kids. Precocious toddlers *respond* there to low-slung sun dresses in hot orange and Mexican pink. Six-year-olds, their appetites whetted by the telly ads, gravitate with swinging hips towards minuscule bikinis in the vibrant shades of a parrot's wing – so redolent of an untouched Rain Forest. In their imagination they are already Supermodels, off to an expenses-paid shoot in Hawaii. And the bubble-gum flavour lip salve is an international bestseller.

Palm Beach rules O.K., but it is a terrible let down for the elderly Australian couple desperately seeking a tweed coat with velvet collar to mail to their grandchild in Melbourne. *Tatler* recently castigated Princess Margaret for sending her daughter to school in one in the 1970s. Buckle My Shoe, once Harvey Nichols' Children's shoes, has branched into a baby boutique for sophisticates from nought to twelve. Beside the shoes, which range from jewelled sandals to gold kid lace-ups, hangs an exquisite selection of party and daywear. At time of writing, Sloanish navy and white predominates, but what navy and white – piped and appliquéd, and frilled and edged with costly organza. Young customers arrive in droves to say they are bored with Osh Kosh jeans and washable gear from Mothercare. They finger the organza expertly, flicking over the price tags to check if a number has class.

Over the road at La Cicogna, a fairy-tale cradle frothing with lace, its silken drapes covered with sequin and bead embroidery, is *de rigeur* for all the Arab Royal Families. At £2,700 it is also popular with rich Japanese. Europe's arch-priest of style for children, Gianni Puccio, opened his London boutique fifteen years ago. In Italy there are now nine branches of La Cicogna, and his name is a household word. He enticed Eve Freshwater away from Browns of South Molton Street to be the Buyer for his London shop. 'Our customers know what they want from four years old,' she says 'and they want what Mother wears – Moschino, Armani and, of course, Gianni Versace.'

All the top Italian houses now design babyclothes, and London is following suit. Already you can buy a Joseph babygrow. A granny from New York, who'd been in the rag trade all her life, stopped by to drool over the christening robes in pale pink duchess silk embroidered with seed pearls and a snip at £255. She wanted a suit for a little boy's Bar Mitzvah. A seven year old in a baseball cap came in. She walked straight over to Armani Junior and picked out a day dress at a modest £92. The American lady shook her head. 'Yeah,' she said wisely, 'Some husband's going to suffer.'

19

A Hotbed of Sin

No account of Knightsbridge would be complete without a peep inside the London Oratory. Looking at it today with its glorious blue and gold Sanctuary, its Lady Chapel ablaze with votive candles and its vergers resplendent in tail coats of the subtlest olive green, it is hard to imagine the battles which raged at its foundation. Correctly styled the Church of Our Lady and St Philip Neri, its nickname of 'the Brompton Oratory' has stuck, and nowadays it is even listed as such in the London telephone directory. Newman would have been livid, for as we mentioned earlier, he despised Brompton as a suburb of second-rate gentry and second-rate shops.

When the Oratorians moved there it wasn't even that. It was full of muddy lanes, leading to dairy farms and market gardens. It lay half a mile from Knightsbridge Green. Brompton Row came to an end there, and the country road to Fulham, a foul place known for its smelly drains, branched off to the left. Stigmatised even by Thackeray, Brompton's only visible asset was the new-built Church of Holy Trinity, and when its Vicar learned the Oratorians were coming, he launched into a furious campaign to stop them. Catholic emancipation was a dominant issue in the 1850s, but not everyone viewed it with unbounded joy.

'Am I Queen of England, or am I not?' cried an outraged Queen Victoria when, as Supreme Head of the Anglican Church, she was informed restoration of the Roman Hierarchy had gone through.

The Oratorians were mostly converts. Their sudden appearance in London in birettas and long black cassocks created something of a stir. Two were spotted in St James's Park feeding the swans. They were *stared* at by the Commissioner of Woods and Forests. *Punch* lampooned them, and their plan to build a church enraged not only the Queen and the Vicar of H.T.B., but also Pugin, Victorian England's leading pundit on ecclesiastical architecture. He had emphatically pronounced the Gothic style *Christian* and the Classical *Pagan*. When the Oratorians built a 240 foot basilica with a dome, and imported a processional Madonna from Italy who changed her vestments with the seasons, the Anglicans knew he was right.

The first premises of the Order were in King William Street off the Strand. The fathers preached to the poor, and took over the Lowther Rooms which had previously been a whisky store. 'Has your Lordship heard that the Oratorians have opened the Lowther Rooms as a Chapel?' wrote Pugin to Lord Shrewsbury. 'A place of violent debauchery. One night a masked ball, next Benediction. What a degradation for Religion.'

Despite Pugin's objections the two oratory houses of London and Birmingham were quickly established. Newman suggested the fathers should build their own HQ first, as it would be easier to raise funds for a church than a house. His deal in Mayfair fell through, so the Community threw themselves on Our Lady's mercy, promising that if *she* would secure a home for them, they would dedicate their new church to her. Just then the Brompton site became vacant. The faithful saw it as a sure sign of Marian intervention. What could poor Newman do? Although his was the guiding intelligence behind the Oratory, when it came to fund-raising, it was Father Faber who had the charisma. Even in the Lowther Street Rooms he knew how to put on a show.

'We had four hundred candles beside crimson satin drapes, and we hung the Sanctuary walls with crimson damask with yellow lace down the seams. Shrubs, flowers and a frontal of gold and silver lace. It took people's breath away,' he wrote of the Oratorians first Forty Hour Service. When they got to Brompton, Faber proved a genius at drawing in the ladies of fashion. 'We get some forty to fifty people to half past four Benediction,' he wrote to Lady Arundel. 'It forms a part of their drive. Lady Fingall says this is the only church where we late dining people can worship God.'

The Oratory has always had tone. The Duke of Norfolk was an immediate benefactor and three of the earliest patrons were pious women, whose coats of arms are appropriately displayed in the clerestory windows; Mrs Bowden, who gave the largest side chapel; Ann, Duchess of Argyll, whose gift of an organ was so munificent that the roof had to be taken off to get it into the building; and Mrs Dalglish-Bellasis, who with her second husband gave the outer dome. The Duchess of Argyll, third wife to the seventh Duke, first came to the church as a penitent. She was so dowdily dressed that the verger sent her packing with the words, 'Father Faber is engaged. Go off to Dr Manning. He is good enough for the likes of you.' Another of Father Faber's admirers stuck £10,000 in cash into the collection box, before going off to become a nun.

The good man worked terribly hard at his sermons and suffered from constant headaches. On one occasion he experienced a miraculous cure, when he pressed a relic of St Mary Magdalene to his temples. The experience shook him to the core, and he must have repeated the story many times, for it was reputedly one of his penitents who endowed the Oratory with a Chapel to St Mary Magdalene. It seems to be dedicated to the wrong saint. Father Faber's headache cure was effected by Mary Magdalene dei Pazzi, a seventeenth century Carmelite nun, but close inspection of the chapel suggests it is dedicated to that early reflexologist, the first century Mary Magdalene, who so kindly massaged Our Lord's feet with expensive ointment. In France she is venerated as the Patron Saint of Fallen Women, and the prostitutes near the Paris Opera have developed a quite separate cult, invoking her to bring them good business. In *English* sanctorals the connection with harlotry is played down. She is simply listed as 'a sinner'.

20

Handy for Harrods

L ADY CELESTRIA NOEL tells a wonderful story about a friend of her mother's, who wanted to buy a flat. Before explaining to the estate agent the size required, the number of bathrooms, or even the price, she stipulated, 'It must be handy for Harrods.'

Basia Briggs, whose first job when she left school was in Harrods' Complaints Department, once went to live in Australia. Surrounded by a vast expanse of bush and endless gum trees, she grew homesick for the rattle of a London taxi. She bred Pekingese to earn her fare home, using 'Knightsbridge' as her kennel name.

Even Sir Dirk Bogarde, who is permanently homesick for Provence, finally settled in a London flat 'a short walk from Harrods'. Perhaps there is something mesmeric about the 11,500 light bulbs which illuminate the mighty façade, or perhaps others shop there, as I do, because they find Accounts less fatiguing than arithmetic.

In his autobiography, *A Traveller's Life*, Eric Newby devotes a whole chapter to 'Travels in Harrods'. His mother was a model girl at the store in 1912. She married a wholesale costumier. Being no mean spender, she went through the Layette Department 'like a combine

Perhaps others shop there, as I do, because they find Accounts less fatiguing than arithmetic.

harvester' at the approach of her first-born. Newby's earliest memories are of his mother telephoning Harrods for a consignment of French sardines in olive oil – on Account, of course.

When he was old enough to have his hair cut at Harrods, Eric's mother would say, 'Hold my hand tight, or you'll get lost.' He did hold tight, for fear of ending in that 'undiscovered country from whose bourne no traveller returns' midway between Overdue Accounts and the Funeral Department, where they corralled lost children, before Accounting moved to the Fifth Floor. After the hated hair-cut, thousands of children have been, and are, rewarded with a visit to Pets. In Newby's time they vetted the parrots to see none of them used bad language.

Later, he recalls the traumatic pilgrimage to Boy's Wear, when at the end of the Summer Holidays, Harrods' catalogue slipped through the letter box, bearing the horrible slogan, 'Back to School'. When he returned to England from a German prisoner-of-war camp in 1945, to lose his clothing coupons on his first day of freedom, he was recognised, even when clad in 'Battledress anti-gas'.

'Dear, dear Sir, we can't have one of our customers without a change of trousers can we?' said an elderly salesman tenderly, 'Mum's the word, but here in Harrods we have more gentlemen's trousers than there are clothing coupons in the whole United Kingdom.'

Things slipped badly in the sixties. They stopped checking the parrots' language. One of my son's early memories of having his hair cut involved trying to see which swore most, a foul-mouthed Harrods' parrot, or the mynah bird which shouted 'Bloody hell' in the aviary of

Derry & Tom's Roof Garden. Pets has always been a source of good stories. A monumentally rich dog-walker, who wishes to remain anonymous once worked there and remembers the day the lion got loose.

'There were two of them, Justin and Christian, cubs really – everyone used to stroke them. They had to be fed at the weekend and I had just slipped downstairs to check some vats of dog food I'd left boiling, when I saw one of the cages was open. I rushed all over the store. Two workmen were mending the roof. I'll never forget their faces when I said, "Excuse me, have you seen a lion walking about?" We found him in the end – having a nice little snooze in the Piano Department.'

The same raconteur was present the day the python exhaled, knocking the front out of its home premises and also when the bushbabies disappeared on a camping holiday.

'We knew they were alive. They kept creeping into Pets at dead of night and helping themselves to bits of pet food from the counter, but we didn't know where they were, until we got a complaint from Lampshades. The buyer found tiny paw marks all over his pleated silks. We explained to him that bushbabies pee on their hands, and leave little sticky finger marks. He threw a fit, "Quick, you must search my whole department." They'd made a sweet little nest for themselves in the bottom of a cardboard box. One of the lampshade salesmen put his hand in and they bit it, but even that wasn't as bad as the time Veronica, the tapir, frightened the cleaning lady in Small Electricals.'

Credit accounts were not allowed at Harrods until

1885. For the first thirty-six years of the store's history, settlements were strictly cash. Charles Digby Harrod, son of the founder, Charles Henry Harrod changed the pattern. Everyone waited with bated breath to see if Royalty would take advantage. Royal credit at that time was a delicate matter. The Duchess of Teck (Queen Mary's mother) had set a shocking example. She was such a spendthrift that Queen Victoria sent her abroad to avoid her creditors, but 'Fat Mary', as the Londoners called her, merely set up a friendship with Miss Burdett-Coutts of the banking family and gave lavish parties in an Italian villa. She once scandalised all Kensington by opening a charity gala to which local store owners had given large donations with the words 'And now I must propose a special note of thanks to Mr John Barker to whom we all *owe so much.*' In the Duchess's case it was the barefaced truth.

Money, of course, was not generally understood by ladies. When the fortunes of the Hanbury-Tracy family crashed in the 1890s, Winifred, Countess of Dysart, a great *aficionado* of Harrods' Hat Department was told by her lawyers that she could not spend any more money, because there was none.

'Oh,' she said quite unworried, 'but I have plenty of cheques.'

Actresses were among the first to benefit from the new credit arrangement. Lillie Langtry and Ellen Terry opened Harrods accounts immediately. In more recent times Ava Gardner, whose film, *The Barefoot Contessa*, billed her as 'the most beautiful animal in the world' bought a flat near the store, where she lived with her Mexican housekeeper and her Welsh corgi, Morgan, until her death in 1990. Her third husband, Frank Sinatra, loved her so much he staged suicide attempts to lure her back, but Knightsbridge offered more home comforts than Beverly Hills. People claimed Ava slept in Ennismore Gardens, but *lived* in Harrods. Jay Morley, the first man to work in Harrods' Perfumery remembers her as a night creature.

'In the morning she'd come in with dark glasses and a belted mack, like any ordinary housewife, then one evening I saw her at Covent Garden Opera. She floated down the staircase in a Balmain cape and a cloud of Mary Chess Tuberose. The audience gasped. She was such a *star*. Lady Diana Cooper was just the same – Beauty that took your breath away. Those ladies were so elegant – none of your slouching in jeans and a T-shirt.'

Jay himself would never have slouched. He had danced at the Folies Bergères with the great Josephine Baker, and later with the Bluebell Girls at the Paris Lido, where deportment was all. He was famed in Perfumery for wearing a pink shirt and a matching carnation. Royal ladies sent him Christmas and birthday cards. He knew more about scent than anyone else in the retail trade. When men came shopping for their wives, he would put them at their ease with stories of the Emperor Napoleon bathing in eau de Cologne on campaign. One morning a shy man in a grey suit approached him. 'And how can I help you, dear boy?' asked Jay sympathetically. The customer looked a little surprised. He was Mohammed Al-Fayed and he had just bought Harrods.

Maybe Mr Al-Fayed looked triumphant. He was the victor in a fight against Lonrho PLC, and even though

Tiny Rowland, Lonrho's Chief Executive, was reluctant to admit defeat, Mr Al-Fayed could reasonably have supposed that morning that he *owned* Harrods. This was to underestimate Knightsbridge Woman, for of course, it is the unquestioning belief of whole battalions of Harrods' customers, that *they* own Harrods. It takes a bold man to set them right.

Roy Miles, the Mayfair art dealer, was once in the store feeling on top of the world. He was wearing a smart blue suit and had a nice silk handkerchief in his pocket, when a peremptory voice said

'Where's the Library?'

A famous salesman in his own right, Mr Miles did not greatly mind being taken for Harrods' staff, but he was *furious* that the customer did not say 'Please.'

'May I know your name, Madam?' he asked pleasantly.

'My name', said the customer, 'is Lady—'

Miles repeated the name thoughtfully, as though wishing to get it absolutely correct. 'Yes,' snapped the woman, 'and do you know *who* I am?'

'Yes, Madam, I know exactly who you are. I'm afraid you're not grand enough to use our Library.' The art dealer bowed politely and went on his way.